Facebook Ads 2019

*The Best Fu*king Guide to Facebook
Advertisement, Retargeting Strategies, and Pixel
Data for a Social Media Marketing Agency,
Dropshipping, E-commerce, and Local Businesses*

Table of Contents

Introduction

Without a doubt, Facebook is one of the biggest internet stars since the internet itself was created - and although the giant social media platform has gone through a lot lately and has been put under a lot of scrutiny, the absolute truth is that Facebook is as strong as ever.

They might be undergoing changes, mostly related to their privacy policies and the way they are explained to users - but even so, Facebook is still home to no less than 2.3 billion users (as of Q4 in 2018). [1]

That means one-third of the world is on Facebook - and if you consider the fact that only about half of the global population is connected to the internet[2], the importance of Facebook in the online landscape grows exponentially.

For most people, Facebook is the blue site you scroll on long procrastination breaks at work, what you open up in the morning after your first cup of coffee, and in many cases, the last thing you check before you go to sleep.

Despite not being at all the first social network ever created, Facebook is the single most successful one. Those of you old enough to remember MySpace will know the difference between Myspace and Facebook - and how, ultimately, Facebook made the experience *simpler*.

---

[1]Facebook users worldwide 2018 | Statista. (2019). Retrieved from https://www.statista.com/statistics/264810/number-of-monthly-active-facebook-users-worldwide/
[2]Global Internet usage. (2019). Retrieved from https://en.wikipedia.org/wiki/Global_Internet_usage

This book is not dedicated to Facebook and the features that make it really easy to use - or the features that make it really popular either.

This book is dedicated to those of you who want to leverage the power of an aptly, intelligently built platform to tap into your target audience of the total 2.3 billion on this platform.

Never before has it been so easy to reach out to such a large and diverse pool of candidates - and never before has it been so easy to granularly target your message to reach the right people. Facebook is a huge player on the ad market online - and their huge base of users, as well as their performant ad platform, are the key ingredients that make this specific social media site the one most marketers jump on when they want to reach out their target audience.

For a beginner, the intricacies of Facebook ads might feel daunting, confusing, and downright anxiety-inducing.

Things are much simpler, though - because Mark Zuckerberg and his amazing team made it happen.

This book is dedicated to those of you who are new to Facebook ads but want to make the very most out of it from day one.

This book is for those of you ready to take on a challenge and transform the way you approach social media marketing, Facebook marketing, and communication in general.

This book is for those of you who are tired of pointless online articles that say absolutely zilch about how to *actually* use Facebook to market your business (or your clients' business).

By the end of the last page in this book, you will have all the tools and knowledge you need to make Facebook advertising easy - but more importantly, the tools and knowledge you need to make Facebook *efficient*.

Thank you for taking the time to read this book. You are about to open the doors to a whole new understanding of how Facebook works, how social media marketing works and, ultimately, how the internet itself works. You are about to open the doors to an age where you can make the absolute most of advertising on the internet - the easy, headache-free, proficient way.

The Basics of Facebook Advertising

Pixels, targeting, audiences, and then some retargeting to top it off - Facebook advertising can very well sound like a foreign language to someone who hasn't really gotten into it. And in all honesty. it is perfectly understandable if you feel overwhelmed.

However, you shouldn't.

In reality, Facebook advertising comes down to a few basic concepts - concepts that might be complex at first, but when you get to understand them, you will be able to build any kind of Facebook ad campaign, for any kind of business.

This chapter is all about the very basics of Facebook advertising - the ins and outs of how Facebook ads work and, more importantly, how to make them work for you.

I will move through the three basic levels of Facebook advertising - this is the absolute foundation of your understanding of how this platform works for advertisers. Then, we will move into understanding the essential terms marketers use when setting up campaigns on Facebook - terms that might seem, as mentioned before, *foreign*, but which really come down to basic marketing know-how. Last, but not least, I will explain how Facebook Business Manager works - the interface Facebook has built to bridge between advertisers and Facebook as an advertising platform.

Without further ado, let's dive into these basics so that you can then proceed to take actual action.

The 3 Levels of Facebook Advertising

Understanding how Facebook advertising works is really simple - it all comes down to the three pillars of how Facebook advertising functions. Mastering these concepts is very important because it will help you go beyond just "copying" what other advertisers are doing. Instead, it will help you go in-depth with your campaigns and customize them according to your particular needs - or your clients' needs if you run a marketing agency.

Please keep in mind that these are the essentials - the brick and mortar of your future campaigns. So, my advice is to take your time to understand them correctly - because once you do that, everything else will come more natural. Even more, understanding these basics will also set you up for success from the very beginning - but the opposite (just glancing over them) will most likely set you up for failure.

Campaigns - The Highest Level

Campaigns are the highest level of Facebook advertising structure - in the sense that this is where you start from. If I had to compare this to building a house, the Campaign level is the very ground upon which you lay the foundation - the parcel of land you are going to use for it. You can build multiple houses on this land, and each of the houses can have different structure, architecture, and appeal.

As you will see, the Campaign level is all about choosing your objective - what you want to achieve with a particular campaign. You can have multiple campaigns on Facebook, and each campaign can have different audiences and multiple ad sets. Basically, you can narrow down and segment your campaigns as much as you need to.

Every Campaign will be centered on one of the three main types of objectives all marketing campaigns (on and off Facebook) should have:

1. Awareness - making people aware that your brand is out there. This is the equivalent of the Top of the Funnel - the very opening of your sales funnel, where you attract a large chunk of visits from people who might be potentially interested in your services.

2. Consideration - drawing part of the people who are already aware of your business further into the funnel and making them *consider* your products or services. On the customer's end, this translates into "making the shortlist" - the moment when customers are actually thinking of buying a product, maybe even adding it to the cart.

3. Conversion - giving a nudge people who are considering buying your product and helping them decide (in your advantage, of course). This is when people make the final call and click "Buy".

Every objective is there to help you coordinate your Facebook ads to your specific strategy. For instance, if you are focused on content, you will naturally want to settle on the type of content that draws most people towards your business - which is most likely video content. In this case, you will want to set Video Views as your main Facebook Ad Campaign Objective.

Retargeting campaigns on Facebook allow you to send visitors from Facebook to your site. For this purpose, you have to pick either Traffic or Conversions as your main objective (and which one you choose depends on what you want people to do: visit your site to create more traffic on it or to attract more people to your site to make a purchase).

Not sure what type of objective is best for you? Well, the very best way to determine this is to de-construct your main marketing goal. For instance, if you want to boost your eCommerce's sales, you will want to create a campaign that offers people a given discount to trigger them to make a buy on your site. To make people actually go to your site to get the discount, you can set a campaign that pushes them to a landing page where they have to opt-in - and in this case, you should choose Conversions as your main campaign objective.

This is just an example - the key tip to take with you here is that the strategy and the purpose of your ads determine the main objective when you set a Campaign on Facebook.

Ad Sets - The Targeting Levels

Once you have decided on the specific Objective of your Facebook campaign, you should move further on to Targeting.

The Targeting level is the second stage of your Campaign setting process. This is where you get granular with your audience and select who you want to target.

This is obviously very important for the success of your campaign - it is the very reason Facebook ads are so valuable and the very reason so many businesses flock to this method of advertising their products.

TV ads used to allow for some sort of targeting - e.g. beer commercials were more likely to perform better during sports shows. But back then, actually measuring the results and getting really granular with your target was not possible.

The internet (with Facebook included) allowed marketers to do this.

The Targeting level will help you be very specific about how your ad will run (or more precisely, who will see it, when, and how much you can spend on this).

Do keep in mind that this campaign stage is absolutely crucial because it will actually specify how your ad will be run. It can actually make or break an entire campaign and it can determine if your Facebook ad investment is successful and yields an expected ROI or if it's just money flushed down the drain.

Here are the basic elements to consider when setting your Targeting in your Campaign on Facebook:

1. The target demographics and their main interests

This is by far one of the easiest ways to target any kind of audience - using their main demographic and interests, you can display ads to those who are likely to be interested in your products. This approach is usually used by businesses when they want to target brand new people who are completely new to their brand.

Let's say, for instance, that you have a shoe-based eCommerce site and you want to draw people's attention to it. Using the target demographics and interests approach, you will set an ad campaign that targets, for example:

- Women (because they are more interested in shoes)

- Located within 100 miles of your depot (because you offer free delivery within that distance)

- Aged between 20 and 40 (because they are more likely to 1. have the funds to make a purchase on your site and 2. shop online)

- Interested in fashion, designers, beauty (because this is the niche most likely to buy a new pair of shoes).

- Have a certain type of income (because, for instance, if you sell luxury shoes, this will be a crucial factor in the buyer's decision process).

Using this approach, Facebook will display your ads to people who fit the aforementioned criteria and it will charge you based on that. You set your budget from the very beginning and it can be as low as $1 - and according to that, Facebook will show it to a given number of people who fit your criteria. Obviously, the more you invest, the more people will see your ad - and the more likely it is that you will boost your sales.

You can set on an audience as large or as small as you want it to be. The very best results are achieved when you layer the criteria to achieve a mixture of them so that you narrow down to the group of people that are truly most inclined to buy your products: your ideal customers.

Under the "Detailed Targeting" section, you can include or exclude certain groups of people - and here's a cool trick to follow here: using the AND condition will help you narrow down your audience even more.

2. People who are already familiar with your business

Another approach you can take to Facebook ad targeting is by aiming for those people who are already at least slightly familiar with your business - more exactly, people who have already interacted with your business online (be it via your website, your Facebook page, or even via the emails you send out for marketing purposes).

These custom audiences can be excellent for retargeting campaigns. Basically, what you are doing here is calling people back to give your business another look at. For instance, if someone entered your website and looked around (even if they only did it for one minute), a retargeting campaign will show them an ad on Facebook following their visit on your site. They will be reminded of you and they will come back to reconsider a purchase there.

These are not people who are new to your business - they already know, and they may even like and interact with your business quite closely. These are the people who are already in the Middle of the Funnel stage (or people who have already bought from your business before and you want to make them return as loyal customers).

When you set the targeting levels according to this approach, you can choose from one of the following categories:

- Website Traffic (people who visited your site - we will get into more detail on how Facebook knows this under the 'How to Install a Facebook Pixel' chapter of this book)

- Customer File (people in your database, which you upload on Facebook's platform and fine-tune for better targeting)

- App Activity (people who interacted with your business via a mobile app)

- Engagement on Facebook (people who liked your business page or engaged with it in any way)

In the last chapter of this book, I will get into more detail on how to use these features to create successful retargeting campaigns, and I will teach you the main tips to keep in mind to make sure your attempts at retargeting existing or near-customers are successful).

3. Lookalike audiences

A Facebook lookalike audience is an audience similar to one that you have already created in your Facebook Business Manager Campaigns.

Or, in other words, you will use lookalike audiences when you want to target people who are very similar in terms of demographics, interests, and behaviors to people you have already (successfully) targeted).

This is an immensely valuable approach when you have already had success with a specific audience and want to tap into more groups of Facebook users that are very similar to those you already had success with.

There are four main types of lookalike audiences you can use when setting a Facebook campaign:

- Video lookalike

Statistics say that Facebook video is really popular. In fact, no less than 30% of Facebook users find video to be one of the best ways to discover new products when they are on this social media channel. [3]

If you have already leveraged the power of Facebook video ads

---

[3]Shifts for 2020: Multisensory multipliers. (2019). Retrieved from
https://www.facebook.com/business/news/insights/shifts-for-2020-multisensory-multipliers

to build brand awareness and create a sense of trustworthiness among your target audience, a video-based lookalike audience will help you "clone" your success on a new audience whose behaviors are very likely to be similar to that which you had success with.

To be able to create a video lookalike audience, you must first create a custom video audience (and run a campaign, to see how well it works for your particular situation and adjust where needed).

The best thing about custom video audiences is that you can actually target people who have watched videos similar to yours - and thus increase your chances that your videos are shown to the people who are likely to actually end up buying from you as well. I will get into more detail on how you can create a custom audience in the next chapter of this book. Furthermore, I will get into more detail on how to create a lookalike audience in the same chapter as well.

- Email lookalike

Email-based lookalike audiences tend to work very well and deliver excellent results - precisely because they are based on the fact that these are already your customers (or at least subscribers who have opted-in to receive your newsletters) - so your chance of success is pretty high.

Same as with video lookalikes, you will first have to set a custom email audience in your Facebook Business Manager so that you can clone this and use if further on.

- Conversion lookalike

This type of lookalike audience will target people who have been on your website and have already been converted (to buying your products, subscribing to your email, or any other specific event you have labeled as a conversion as per your marketing and business strategy).

For example, going back to the shoe eCommerce site mentioned earlier, if you run a lead magnet campaign offering a discount code for purchases on your site, you can create a conversion lookalike audience consisted from people who have already triggered that lead (or in other words, people who have already submitted/agreed to submit some sort of information in exchange for a discount code). Targeting people with similar behaviors will help you push your campaign even further, with less chance that you spend money on something that just doesn't work.

- Page likes lookalike

People who have already liked your page are most probably customers or potential customers in their last decision stage - people who already trust your business and who are already interested in it.

Targeting people who show the same kind of interests as those who have already liked your page means that you will be set up for success from the very beginning of your ad creation process.

Plus, creating a lookalike audience based on your Facebook audience is extremely easy from the point of view of how you can do this. While you have to create custom audiences for all the aforementioned lookalike audiences, you don't have to do this for Page Likes-based audiences (precisely because, well, Facebook already has that data and they don't need you to reiterate it).

The targeting combinations you can make are almost limitless -

no matter what you do and no matter what your main purpose might be with Facebook Ads, you will definitely find the very best solution for your situation and specific needs.

When your audience is in place, you will be required to fill in more information about the campaign you are setting up, such as:

- Ad placement (where on the page you want your ad to be)

- Budget (the exact sum of money you are ready to pay on all of this)

- Schedule (how many days you want to display the ad)

- Bid type (daily, for the entire campaign, and so on).

With all these basics set in place, the next thing you will have to do is...

The Ad - The Actual Promotion

Once you have set up the Campaign Objectives, as well as who you are actually targeting with your campaign, it is time to move on to the built of the actual ad creation process.

No worries, there's no Mad Men big agency involved here - but you do have to have some basic marketing and communication knowledge to be able to create ads that are not only targeted at the right people, but also determine them to take action (in one direction or another, depending on what your goal with this campaign is).

There are two main stages you should follow when creating an ad on Facebook (or really, anywhere else online):

1. Creating it.

This is really a creative work. There's not much to the technicalities behind it, but there are some tips that will help you get the right message across to your target audience and determine them to take action:

- Keep in mind that visuals are crucial. Facebook and social media (and truly, all of the internet) are very visual. So, the photo you use for your specific ad campaign should be very attractive - both from an aesthetic point of view and from a content one.

- Your ad should be relevant. The photo should be relevant. The text itself should be relevant too. For instance, if your ad promotes a discount code for shoes, you shouldn't post pictures of a tractor and advertise a discount code for *everything on your site.*

- Its value proposition is clear. In simple terms, the value proposition is the *why* your target audience would click on the ad and land on your site. Be very clear about what people will get when they click: access to a discount, access to a product, information, etc.

- If it's a video ad, it shouldn't be too long. People don't like long ads, even when they are great. They will either disengage when they feel an ad is too long or they will skip entirely.

- Its call to action is very catchy. Try to go beyond the basics with this, because it can make all the difference in the world. Think of a smart call to action that actually suits your business purpose, your target audience or your brand.

2. Testing it.

No matter how much research you do and how well you know your target audience, testing your ads is still very much necessary because it will help you settle on versions of an ad that show the very best results.

There are three major components you can A/B test with relation to a Facebook ad:

- You can test the copy. This test should be run when you have multiple options for your copy and you want to see which one performs the best

- You can test the image. This test can be very important when you have two different images/ graphics because they can have paramount importance in the way your target audience perceives your ad. Split testing them will allow you to settle on that which works best

- You can test the ad format. Facebook offers various types of ads (as you will see described in the chapter entitled "The Science and Art of Creating a Facebook Ad Campaign"). Split testing the different formats will allow you to see if, for example, a carousel ad works best on your audience than a video ad.

Don't be afraid to test your ads - it might seem that you are spending more money, but in reality, this will actually help you boost conversion rates on the money you are already investing, leading to a higher ROI.

In fact, I will extrapolate this to everything connected to digital marketing in general: it is all about trial and error, testing and choosing. Regardless of where you place your ads or if you want to achieve everything organically, the ability to try, fail, and test lies at the very basis of online marketing.

Whoever says they have a recipe that works 100% for everyone is, well, completely lying. What you should rely on is your own knowledge - and this book is focused on offering you the know-how, so that you can make the absolute most out of your Facebook ads.

Understanding Facebook Ad Vocabulary

As mentioned before, for those of you who are brand new to Facebook Ads, the ad vocabulary might sound like plain and simple (or, well, not so simple) gibberish.

Things are far simpler than they seem, though. Here are the basic terms to keep in mind when it comes to Facebook Ads:

1. Custom audience. This is a feature used for Facebook ads, which allows you you to create an audience that fits your selected set if criteria. For instance, in the example we previously offered with the eCommerce selling shoes, you could create multiple custom audiences:

    - One for the higher priced products on your site

    - One for the low priced products on your site

    - One for the bags you might be selling on your site

Creating a custom audience has two main advantages:

    - You can easily access them when you set up a new campaign (so you will not have to go through the criteria selection process all over again);

    - You can use them when you are creating lookalike audiences.

2. The Facebook Pixel. No, this has nothing to do with actual design, photo pixels, or anything similar. The Facebook pixel is a line of code you add to your site (you can do it with zero web development knowledge)) and which will track who visits your site (and connect that

22

information with Facebook Ads), as well as what people do on your site (e.g. if they visit a specific page, for instance).

3. Lookalike audience. As mentioned before, a lookalike audience is the custom audience you create based on the features that are similar to those of a previous campaign that worked for you. These lookalike audiences are created automatically upon request, so that you can tap into an audience that is similar to one which has successfully responded to your campaigns before.

4. Data point attributes. These are the actual specificities you mean to target with your campaign - the user information that is used to create campaigns and target an audience that is a good fit for your specific product.

5. Retargeting event codes. These are tracking signals that will help you create campaigns for when customers get to specific parts of a website/ different stages of the sales funnel (e.g. viewing content can be one retargeting event code, adding to cart is another event, a purchase is another event, and so on).

These terms are very important because they lie at the very basis of why Facebook is so valuable: it allows you to target very specific audiences, it allows you to find audiences that are similar to those which you have already targeted, and it allows you to achieve actual success with your campaigns.

Understanding Facebook Business Manager

Facebook Business Manager is the interface between you and Facebook - it is your studio and your laboratory at the same time.

Understanding this part of your Facebook account is extremely important because this is your "home" - the place where your campaigns will happen and the place where you will launch your ideas from. The place where the success of your Facebook ads will happen.

Beyond your actual ad accounts, the Facebook Business Manager will also allow you to manage the Pages you have created, as well as the people associated with them (the people you have assigned with your social media daily posts, for example).

The main reason Facebook Business Manager is such a great tool is that it makes it marketing easy to do on Facebook, precisely because it brings everything into one place. This is where all of your Facebook marketing and advertising activities will spring from - so it is essential that you understand it and that you use it correctly so that you can pull all your marketing ideas in one place and launch them into cyberspace. Furthermore, this management page allows you to manage your Instagram account, as well as product catalogs.

Last, but definitely not least, your Facebook Business Manager is the place where you centralize your data and generate relevant reports to help you and your team members gain a better understanding of what works and what doesn't with the marketing campaigns you have launched until now.

Many of you might have put off the creation of the Facebook Business Manager account because you might not have known what it is and what it is actually used for.

If that is the case, follow these steps to set up your Facebook Business Manager as soon as possible:

1. Actually creating the account

Even if you already have a Facebook page, you can still create your Facebook Business Manager account:

- Visit business.Facebook.com

- Click on the button that says "Create Account" (it's a blue button at the top left side of the screen)

- Type your business name in the box that will pop up

- Click "Continue"

- Enter the contact information you want to use when you manage your Facebook Business Account (name and business email address)

- Click "Finish"

2. Include your business pages

There are a few different things you can do here: you can add a Facebook business page that already exists, or you can create a new one. If you have an agency and you run Facebook marketing for your clients too, you can also ask them to give you access, so that you can add them here.

It is quite important to Request Access, as opposed to Add Page. If you just *add* your clients' pages, they will end up having limited access to these - and that's something no business wants (also, a surefire way to create unpleasant situations between you and your clients).

So, to add a page to your Facebook Business Manager, go to the main dashboard, and:

- Click on "Add Page" from the three options that appear in the center of the screen

- Click "Add Page" again

- Start writing the name of the Facebook page you want to add - it should autocomplete at some point, so you can just select it.

- Click "Add Page"

Please keep in mind that the request you make now will be automatically approved only if you are an administrator on that page. Otherwise, you will have to wait for the approval to come from the administrator of the page.

Also, if you have to add multiple pages, follow the same steps all over again. Facebook Business Manager will allow you to add a bunch of pages so that you can have all of them in one place.

3. Connect your Facebook Ad account

Please keep in mind that Ad accounts that have been added in Facebook Business Manager cannot be removed from there. Furthermore, if you add client ad accounts, do it by using the Request Access feature - this is very important.

If you have already used the Facebook ads, you can simply copy and paste the link to those accounts.

To connect your existing Facebook add account(s) to your

Facebook Business Manager, follow these steps:

- Go to the Facebook Business Manager

- Click on "Add Ad Account" and then on "Add Ad Account again".

- Enter the ad account ID (you will find it in your ad account, in Ads Manager to be more specific).

If you don't have an ad account just yet, follow these steps instead:

- Goto the Facebook Business Manager dashboard

- Click on "Add Ad Account"

- Click on "Create Account"

Do keep in mind the fact that every business can only create one ad account when they are starting out. Once you start to spend actual money with that account, you will be allowed to add up to four more accounts. Even so, you can never add more than five ad accounts in one Facebook Business Manager account.

4. Connect your team

Facebook Business Manager allows you to add members of your team to your account as well so that they can help with the management of all the Facebook assets.

This is, again, a great opportunity to have everything and everyone in one place - which can be paramountly important when you have a lot to handle (and trust me, you *will* end up having a lot to handle once you set up your campaigns and your ads, even if they're for *one* ad account only).

To connect your team to your Facebook Business Manager page, follow these steps:

- Go to the Business Manager dashboard

- Click on the little gear icon at the top of the page

- Click on the tab called "People and assets"

- Choose "People" from the column on the left side of the page. At this point, you will see a list of all the users whom you have granted access to your Facebook Business Manager (or you will only see yourself if this is brand new for you and you haven't added anyone to your team)

- Click on the "Add" button - this will allow you to add members for your Facebook Business Manager account

- A pop-up box will appear - enter the email addresses of the team members you want to connect to your Facebook Business Manager account

- Decide on whether you want to give your team members limited access (by choosing "Employee privileges" or plain and simply full access (by choosing "Admin" privileges).

- Click on the "Add People" button

This section of Facebook Business Manager also allows you to select which of the pages you want which of the team members to be able to work on. For instance, if you have hired a freelance social media manager and you only want them to work on your business page, not on your clients', you will be able to do this here.

There are five basic types of roles your team can take:

- Page admin: this will give your team members access to manage all the aspects of a given page (including, but not limited to actually assigning other page roles to other team members as well)

- Page moderator: this will give your team members access to manage ads, as well as any type of branded content you might want to add to your marketing campaigns. Moderators can also send and delete messages and comments, and they also have access to Page Insights

- Page analyst: this role is somewhat limited, but it will allow the person assigned on it to manage the settings behind your branded content, as well as view Page Insights

- Page editor: team members assigned on this role are similar to page moderators, but they can also publish as the page (which moderators cannot do)

- Page advertiser: this role will give your team member access to do everything analysts do, with the exception that they will be able to create ads as well.

Once you make the selection, just click on the "Next" button.

Do keep in mind that the same roles and the access levels associated with them will fall on the Instagram accounts connected to your Facebook Business Manager as well.

If you want to assign certain people on specific accounts connected to your Business Manager, you will be prompted with a page that allows you to do this as soon as you add team members to the Business Manager account.

Here too, you will have to choose between different roles each team member can have on your page:

- Ad account admin: this person will be able to manage all aspects connected to the campaigns you launch, including to edit billing details, as well as assign roles to other team members

- Ad account analyst: this person will only be able to view the ad performance

- Ad account advertiser: this person will be able to see, edit, as well as create any kind of new ads

Once you have assigned these roles as well, you should click "Next". You will then be prompted to a page that will allow you to assign people on specific catalogs. However, this stage can be skipped if you don't have catalogues (you simply click the "Skip" button).

To make sure you have assigned the right people to the right roles, Facebook will then prompt you a page where you can see how many people you have added to your Facebook Business Manager team, as well as the roles they have been assigned on.

Keep in mind that this process will only send invitations to each member you have added to your team - in order for them to actually be able to work on your pages and campaigns, they will have to accept the invitation as well. Facebook Business Manager will automatically send them an email in this respect - but writing them in person might be a good idea too (because people frequently ignore Facebook notifications like these, and because some of them might not even fully get them properly).

Once assigned in your Facebook Business Manager, a team member can be removed as well. During the pending for approval stage, you will also see all the team invitations you have sent out and you can also withdraw them at any moment if the team members do not respond.

If you want to revoke permission for a team member (e.g. they stop working with your company), you can follow these steps to make it happen:

- Go to the Business Manager dashboard

- Click on the little gear icon located at the top right side of the page

- Go to the "People and Assets" tab

- Click on "People"

- Click on the person you want to remove

- Click "Remove"

5. Connect your partners

If you have partners that might need access to your Facebook Business Manager or simply if you have hired an ad agency to design the campaigns for you, you will have to add them to your Facebook Business Manager account too.

You already know the drill:

- Go to the Business Manager dashboard

- Click on the little gear icon

- Click on the tab called "People and Assets"

- Select the ad account or Facebook page you want the partner to be assigned on

- Click on "Partners" (you will find this in the column on the left side)

- Click on "Assign Partner"

- Choose a suitable role

- You will get a link - copy that and paste it to your partner or agency to invite them to your Facebook Business Manager

- Click on "Close"

6. Connect your Instagram

As you might know it, Facebook and Instagram are basically connected to each other since Facebook acquired Instagram a few years ago.

Connecting your Instagram to your Facebook Business Manager allows you to manage your Instagram campaigns from the same center as you do with the Facebook campaigns, thus simplifying your job and making things easier to track for everyone involved.

To connect your Instagram account, follow these steps:

- Go to your Business Manager dashboard

- Click on the gear icon

- Go to the "People and Assets" tab

- Click on "Instagram Accounts"

- Click "Add"

- Enter your Instagram information

- Click "Next"

- If you have more than one ad accounts in your Facebook Business Manager, you will be prompted to choose which ones are to be connected to your Instagram account

- Click "Next"

- Click "Done" when you get the confirmation pop-up

Your Facebook Business Manager is about so much more than just bringing all your Facebook (and Instagram) assets in one place - this is where you will create a Facebook Pixel from as well.

This is the very HQ of all your efforts on Facebook. This is where you create and monitor ad campaigns, this is where you update your page, this is where you track the activity on your page and the insights provided by this activity, and so on.

The Facebook Business Manager dashboard is divided in five main categories, as follows:

- Plan

- Create & Manage

- Measure & Report

- Assets

- Settings

These five categories are pretty self-explanatory and easy to use - in the end, Facebook Business Manager was created for no other purpose than to make things simple for business owners, agencies, and marketers alike.

In the following chapters, I will show you how to create a proper audience list for your Facebook ads, how to create a lookalike audience, and how to understand the true marketing objective lying at the creation of every ad you let out into cyberspace.

I will then tell you a couple of interesting stories about creating Facebook ad campaigns that truly work, how to install a Facebook Pixel, and how to use Facebook Retargeting to make it *happen* for you too.

Stick around, because the fun has just started!

Creating an Audience List for Facebook Ads

Do you want to know the secret to great Facebook ad campaigns?

Well, there's no actual secret - it all lies in how you set up your campaigns from the very beginning and how you send your message across Facebook as a channel of communication.

If I had to narrow it down to *one* "secret", it would definitely be the creation of an audience list.

This is incredibly important, and here are a few reasons to convince you that you should put some serious thought into the creation of your ads' future audience(s):

- The major advantage of Facebook and advertising on Facebook lies precisely in the way they collect data and use it to help advertisers and marketer reach their target audience.

- The more granular you are with your target audience selection, the more likely it is that your investment will yield the expected ROI

- It's fun. It really is. Once you learn how to work with audiences on Facebook, you will uncover a whole new world of opportunities in terms of the kinds of ads you can use and how to make them really work for your business.

It doesn't even matter what kind of business you run or want to help. It can be Amazon itself or it can be a local pastry shop looking to reach more pastry aficionados in the area and the surrounding areas. Facebook audiences will help you reach precisely to those people who are actually likely to buy your products.

Let's compare this with traditional advertising for a second.

In traditional advertising, you do have some sort of targeting options available. For instance:

- In TV advertising, you can show ads for men's products during sports games because men are more likely to watch these shows, but that doesn't mean that men are the only ones watching these shows. In fact, even if that is actually true, studies show that men pay little to no attention to the ads displayed during a game[4] - they are more interested in the play itself than the ads placed around the football field, and they are more likely to leave the TV during the ad sessions (or just switch the channel around).

- In newspaper advertising, you can somewhat target your ads, especially in terms of local businesses (for instance, you wouldn't set up an ad for your local bakery in the national newspaper). Likewise, ads are more likely to be displayed on those pages which your target audience shows more interest in.

- In billboard advertising, targeting can be achieved as well - but it is not always pursued. Think of what people think of when they are on the highway and of the last three ads you saw on a highway billboard - chances are

---

[4] (2019). Retrieved from
https://www.researchgate.net/publication/254298719_Men_Women_and_S
ports_Audience_Experiences_and_Effects

the two aren't connected. One example of good targeting in billboard advertising is when restaurants advertise their business on highways - people are likely to be hungry when driving for long distances, so they are also likely to stop by and grab a burger.

Traditional advertising is not completely foreign to the concept of targeting - and targeting is in no way a concept that was invented in the digital marketing age.

However, digital marketing has pushed this farther than ever before by allowing people to granularly target the audiences that will actually love your products.

You wouldn't advertise a meat burger to vegans, right?

So why would your hard paid Facebook ads reach people who have zero interest in what you have to offer?

Creating Facebook audiences is truly one of the very best things you can do for your advertising campaigns - and Facebook Business Manager makes it actually easy for you to set up an audience you can use again and again for different campaigns.

How to Create an Audience List for Facebook Ads

Creating an audience list for your Facebook ads is quite easy once you get the gist.

The possibilities in terms of targeting are, as you will definitely notice, *limitless*. You can make it really specific and you can target people who are genuinely interested in what you have to offer (yes, I know I've said this before, but this is the key ingredient to why Facebook ads are so successful and why people keep investing in this).

The basics of how to create an audience list for your Facebook ads are really simple:

1. Go to your Facebook Business Manager dashboard

2. Click on the three horizontal lines/menu on the top left side of the screen

3. Go to the "Assets" tab

4. Click on "Audiences"

5. Scroll down

6. Click on "Create a Custom Audience"

7. At this point, you will have multiple options available to create a custom audience:

    A. Use external sources:

        a. Upload a customer file

You can upload a customer file with your database of customers. This works particularly well for eCommerce businesses because, by their nature, they already have (or are in the process of creating) a list of clients. Every time you buy something online, you will be prompted to sign in to that specific site - and, with your agreement (because GDPR requires it), you will be added to a list of customers.

This type of custom audience list is extremely helpful during special events - such as Black Friday, for example. Not only will you be able to reach out to potential new clients, but, by displaying ads to those who are already your customers, you can loyalize them.

Even more, you can even create ads that offer special discounts for those who are already customers - these ads would only be displayed to your customer file contacts, which means that they are 100% already your clients.

There's a truly large spectrum of ideas you can incorporate with customer files - all it takes is having the right mindset and keeping in mind why you are doing this in the end.

DO keep in mind the fact that Facebook will not allow you to upload a customer list until you have already run a few campaigns on their ad platform and proved that you can actually adhere to their policies.

b. Use your website's traffic

As also mentioned at the beginning of the book, you can create an audience list based on your website traffic.

This is a priceless option, really.

You can use it in a variety of ways:

- to target people who have visited your site and left

- to target people who have left products in the basket

- to target people who looked around your site on specific products

- to remind people of special discounts after visiting your site

- to answer questions you might intuitively think your recent site visitors had (e.g. how your services work, for example)

The sky's the limit here - and I mean it!

Website-traffic based audiences are based on the Facebook pixel you will install on your site - which I will show you how to do later on in the book (I promise it's much easier than it sounds!).

Going back to how you can use site traffic to leverage Facebook ads to your advantage, there's one rule you must follow: your ads will always have to be somewhat connected to your visitors' experience on your site. Therefore, both the image and the copy you use for this kind of ads should be coordinated into the way your visitors interacted with your site.

And yes, Facebook will actually allow you to narrow your audience *that* much.

c. Use app activity

This is a less commonly used method to create an audience list, but it can work in a variety of contexts.

For instance, let's say you have an online bookstore and you offer people an app that allows them to add quotes, book reading ideas, and reviews. If someone interacts with your app by adding a new book to their to-read list, you can display ads that will remind them of that book.

The reason app activity-based audiences aren't as common is because having an actual app or game is not that common with smaller businesses - and small businesses (as well as local businesses) are a huge player on the Facebook ad market.

d. Use offline data

This feature is relatively unknown in the audience creation section of Facebook Ad Manager, but it can be really useful in certain situations.

What exactly is "offline data" considered to be?

Well, for instance, if your business determines actual steps to be made, this could be an offline event Facebook uses for displaying ads.

Furthermore, if someone visited your brick and mortar store, you can use that in this category as well.

Likewise, if someone attended an actual offline event you held, you can include them in this category.

To be able to create this kind of Facebook audience, you will first have to create an Offline Events set. You can do this from the "Offline Events Set" option available in the Facebook Business Manager menu. You will have to name your events set and you will also have to give it a description, and then you will have to update offline data (in CSV format).

This type of audience can be really useful for businesses who run events or operations offline and want to further their efforts in the online world as well.

B. Use Facebook's sources

Want to target people who have liked your Facebook page, or maybe just laughed at a meme you posted on your business page?

You can do that! Given that the information upon which such a list is created is very "local" (in the sense that it already exists in Facebook's database), it would only make sense that they would offer this option.

In general, these kind of audience lists are best when you want to target middle of the funnel and recurrent customers. Because they have already interacted with your page on Facebook, it is likely that the people falling in this category are already considering buying from you (or considering buying from you *again*, for that matter). Giving them a nudge with a Facebook ad might be the missing piece of the buyers' process puzzle.

Ads Manager will provide you with six options in this section:

- Video (audience created based on people who interacted with your videos)

- Lead form (audience created based on people who interacted with a lead form you created on Facebook)

- Instant Experience (audience created based on people who interacted with your Instant Experience on Facebook or Instagram)

- Instagram business profile (audience created based on people who interacted with your Instagram)

- Events (audience created based on people who interacted with your Facebook Events)

- Facebook Page (audience created based on people who interacted with your Facebook Page).

As you can see, you have a really large number of options when it comes to creating audiences on Facebook. There's no "right" or "wrong" type of custom audience, though - it is all based on what your business needs are and what you plan to achieve with your marketing and advertising campaigns on Facebook. Or, in other words, it is all based on your precise objective - a topic I will approach in the last section of this chapter so that you can better understand what an objective is and why it is so important for your Facebook ads.

Creating a Lookalike Audience

As mentioned at the beginning of this book, lookalike audiences are audiences you create on Facebook based on audiences you have already set in place and which have proven results for you.

To help you better understand how a lookalike audience works, imagine you are the owner of a local pet shop and you create an audience based on people who have liked your "We LOVE Cats" Page (a page you created with the sole purpose of building a community around your pet shop as a cat lover).

If that audience has proven results for you, you might want to create a new campaign and tap into the same kind of pool of users. You also want to make sure the new audience will show your ads to different people than your original one so that you can maximize the power of your ads.

This is where a lookalike audience comes in, allowing you to basically "clone" an already successful audience and find new people with the same kind of traits as your original audience included.

There are a million ways to use this extremely powerful tool - and its main advantage is that it will use a "success recipe" you have found and continuously help you find new people who might be interested in your products.

To create a lookalike audience, follow these steps:

1. Go to your Business Manager dashboard

2. Go to the "Asset" tab

3. Click on "Audiences"

4. Select "Create a Lookalike Audience"

5. Select the audience you want to clone

6. Select the location of your audience

7. Select the number of lookalike audiences you want to create (from 1 to 6)

8. Select the percentage of how much of this audience should resemble the older one. For instance, a 1% selection here will give you an audience that is extremely similar to the audience you are cloning. A 10% selection is the maximum you can do here, and it will create an audience that is broader than the "cloned" one.

Creating a Custom Lookalike Audience with LTV

This is a fairly new option offered by Ads Manager, released in 2017 and not frequently talked about - but it is one of those options that can be a true gold mine for eCommerce owners.

Put in very basic terms, LTV is the customer's lifetime value - or, in other words, how much time a customer has spent on your site. This type of audience selection is a bit more complex to understand than the other types of audiences, precisely because it brings in a completely new approach to audiences and how eCommerce businesses can make use of them.

Adding the LTV dimension to your audiences is extremely advantageous step because it will allow you to target those precise people who have spent a lot (or not a lot) on your site. Consequently, you will have the ability to create campaigns that are meant to retain, loyalize, or even evangelize your existing customers.

DO keep in mind that you need to have the data available. Depending on what platform your eCommerce website is built on, you might be able to draw this data directly from your site (sometimes by using the platform's features directly, and other times by using plugins or extensions that allow you to analyze and filter this kind of data).

It is also important to keep in mind that Facebook Ads Manager will only allow you to upload LSV data according to a given format - a template of which you can download when you set up your LSV audience.

To create a custom audience with LSV, follow these steps:

1. Go to your Business Manager dashboard

2. Go to the "Asset" tab

3. Click on "Audiences"

4. Click on "Get Started" on the banner in the middle of the screen (under "New! Use LTV for Better Performing Lookalikes")

5. The first step is preparing a file with your customer data. You can either settle on a set of 15 identifiers (all of which are listed there, as well as explained when you hover over each of them) or you can settle on a 1 customer value.

6. The second step is to upload your file. Before you do this, you will have to download the template and make sure it matches your file. Also, you will have to select the source of this information.

7. The third step is to name your audience. In general, when naming your audience, you want to make sure you are very clear about it so that you can correctly and accurately track it whenever you will need it.

LSV lookalike audiences are incredibly valuable because they will allow you to base your entire Facebook approach on actual data, rather than presumptions - which has grown to be monumentally important for eCommerce businesses who want to achieve actual growth.

Understanding the Marketing Objective

As mentioned in the first chapter of this book, your marketing objective is the secret key to opening the gates of true success with Facebook ads.

Basically, your marketing objective is the Northern Star of your Facebook ad efforts - the guiding light that will allow you to make the best selections during the audience creation, campaign creation, and ad creation processes.

Not only can this be the catalyst of your success, but it can also be the absolute worst enemy too. In fact, the marketing objective is what most people get wrong - and then end up ditching Facebook ads as inefficient, when, in fact, they were on the wrong path from the very beginning.

So, how do you understand your marketing objective?

It all starts with understanding the basic sales funnel.

There are multiple shapes and forms the funnel has taken over the years, but in the end, it all narrows down to three main stages at which your target audience might be in the buying process:

1. Phase One. They are not aware of your existence. At this point, they are either looking for a general product (e.g. shoes), specific product (e.g. Louboutin knockoffs), or simply wandering around the internet, not looking for something specific). This phase is frequently referred to as the "base of the sales funnel" - the large opening that attracts a wide range of potential customers in it.

Your main purpose here is to draw these people further down

the sales funnel - to make them enter your site, take a look at your products, and enter the consideration phase (the middle of the funnel).

2. Phase Two. At this point, your customer has already taken a look at your site. Some of them have just looked around. Others, however, might have even added your product to the basket and they were on the way to the checkout when something made them change their minds. The first group of people is a classic case of "middle of the funnel" users. The second, however, can be either considered in the "middle of the funnel", or they can be considered as "dropouts" (meaning that they have disengaged from your sales funnel and they have dropped out of it).

Your main goal here should be pushing these people towards the checkout and making sure they don't drop out of the funnel (again).

3. Phase Three. At this point, people are very close to making the transaction - so you need to convince them to actually enter their credit card details and make the purchase.

In general, this phase, the tip of the funnel, is not about marketing per se, but about making it easy for your potential buyers to actually...buy. This is tightly connected into the way your site is built, ease of access, and other similar factors that encourage people to offer their money for your products.

Your Facebook ad campaign goals should be tied into these sales funnel phases and the motivations that make people proceed to the next stage (or leave the sales funnel, for that matter).

As I was saying earlier in the book, there are three main objectives you can select in Ads Manager:

1. Awareness

This is all about generating interest in your target audience - it's all about the very broadly-targeted content that will attract a generous influx of people towards your business' sales funnel.

Facebook Ads Manager will allow you to choose from the following awareness objectives:

- Brand Awareness. This objective should be used when you want to raise awareness for your company and the products you sell. When you use this goal, you don't necessarily want people to interact with your content - you don't want clicks, shares, like the content. You just want them to be aware that you exist, you want them to have you in their minds.

In general, brand awareness campaigns are not particularly suitable for smaller businesses that might not have a large budget. Because the end result of a campaign set with this goal is not an actual purchase (or even web traffic or lead generation), you might want to skip the idea altogether. Most of the times, brand awareness campaigns in this context are used by very large companies - such as Coca-Cola, for example.

- Brand Reach. This objective should be used when you want your Facebook ads to be seen by a large number of people but within your target audience and specific budget.

Generally speaking, this type of objective is geared at smaller audiences, when your priority as a business is to reach out to as many people as possible. As a secondary purpose, you want these people to also visit your site, to watch your video, or eventually create a conversion event on your site.

Most times, the brand reach objective is used by marketers who don't want to narrow down their options by a lot, but who still want to make sure their ads will be seen by the right people.

2. Consideration

This is about making people want to look closer at your business. In offline retail, it is the equivalent of a sign that attracts people in the actual store, as opposed to leaving them in the "window shopping" phase.

These are the main types of Consideration objectives you can choose from on Facebook:

- Traffic. This is to be used when you want to push traffic outside of Facebook (such as to your website's blog, a landing page, a podcast episode, etc.). When using this type of objective, Facebook will show your ad to people who are very probable to actually click on the link. The way Facebook will know they are likely to take actual action and engaged is because it will base this assumption on previous behavior.

Do keep in mind that if your final purpose is to make people want to register to a newsletter, or make an actual purchase, this is not the goal you should choose (and you should look under "Conversions", rather than "Consideration").

- Engagement. This objective is somewhat similar to the Traffic one, with the exception that the action you want your audience to take is to like, share, or react to your ad.

This might bring value to those of you who need more page likes, who want more people to respond to an event, and so on. Consequently, your purpose here is to attract a fanbase or a group of people who are interested in your business and will generate more reach in an organic way.

- App Installs. This objective should be used by those of you who have an app and want to download the app.

- Video Views. This objective should be used when you want to promote a video and want to make more people watch it, and then click on a link you give them/ create a conversion.

This can be a very good objective when you know you will want to retarget a video-viewing audience in the future because it will create the foundation of that future retargeting campaign.

DO keep in mind that you shouldn't use the video objective every time you create a video ad. If your ad's purpose is that of leading people to your site, your goal should be Traffic, not Video Views.

- Lead generation. This objective should and could be used when you want to create leads on Facebook without users actually leaving the social network. Facebook Lead Generation will help you collect names, emails, addresses, phone numbers, and other types of basic information. The Facebook Lead Generation tool will help your users auto-fill the forms so that they find it easy to submit it.

In general, using Lead ads means you will have to use another tool (outside of Facebook) to automatically input all the data you are collecting on your Facebook in your email marketing software.

3. Conversions.

If you want to set Conversions as your main goal, do keep in mind that you will have to record a minimum of about 15-25 conversions every week so that Facebook has sufficient data to analyze the people who do convert, and then select those people in your target audience who are most likely to convert. Also, remember that 15-25 conversions are considered to be the absolute minimum and that the data collected based on this number of conversions might not be fully accurate. Ideally, you want to have about 50-100 conversions to provide Facebook with truly relevant data to analyze.

Furthermore, if your traffic/conversion ratio is low (due to the nature of your products or services, such as in the case of a luxury eCommerce store), you might want to avoid the Conversions goal altogether. Instead, you might want to choose the Traffic objective (even if your main purpose is to make people visit your site so that they opt-in or purchase). In these cases, the Conversion objective will do nothing else than limit your reach because there is insufficient data available.

Aside from the Conversions goal per se, this section will also feature two more options:

- Product Catalog Sales. This objective is valuable for eCommerce businesses who want to promote specific products off their product catalog. To be able to use this objective, you will have to integrate your product catalog with Facebook.

- Store visits. This objective is used when you have more than one business location and want to promote your target audience's closest location. To make use of this objective, you will have to set up your business locations in Facebook Business Manager.

A good example of how this can be used is a McDonald's restaurant. If you want to show people the closest McDonald's so that you can attract them to the store, you will use the Store Visits objective.

The Marketing Objective behind a Facebook campaign might sound quite confusing - but it all comes down to that basic Sales Funnel I described above. My advice is to take it into consideration not only when creating Facebook ads, but when creating any kind of content or marketing campaign online.

To find the most suitable Marketing Objective for your specific campaign, you will have to take the Sales Funnel into consideration, but you will also have to consider the nature of your business. It is not always that the most obvious Marketing Objective is also the correct one to choose (like I showed in the Conversions example in the case of a luxury eCommerce).

Think things through - this journey into Facebook ads is, in the end, a learning curve. You must take your time to understand the basic concepts, so that you can decide on what is best for your business, for your target audience, and for the main purpose behind the *why* you are doing Facebook ads.

How to Install a Facebook Pixel

The Facebook pixel is one of those concepts that sound very complicated and might scare you off, especially if you are a beginner.

To be scared of the Facebook pixel would be, however, a big mistake - and from two main points of view.

1. It's actually easy. Yes, I know it sounds like a boogieman and that it sounds like you absolutely have to have development and coding knowledge to install it on your site. However, even people who have absolutely ZERO experience in coding (any language) will be able to install this correctly - and then check to see if it works.

2. It's extremely, extremely powerful. And if you're wondering why, think of all the times you visited a site, looked at a pair of shoes or a tie, and then saw ads of those products everywhere on Facebook until you eventually ended up buying it/ them. Now, that's Facebook pixel working to make sure you don't forget about a specific business.

The Facebook pixel is, at least partly, the root of the Facebook scandal in 2018 as well. Together with cookies, the Facebook Pixel collects data from users when they are on Facebook, as well as when they are off-Facebook, providing marketers and advertisers with the opportunity to use all that data to their advantage.

There are three main ways to use the Facebook pixel:

1. To create custom audiences (as shown previously in this book)

2. To create lookalike audiences (as also shown previously)

3. To create retargeting campaigns (as I will show you in the next chapter)

Can that much information be used to create a negative influence?

Without a doubt, yes. But I am not here to discuss the morality or ethicality of the Facebook pixel and the transparency with which Facebook lets its users know they are "tracked".

I am here to show you that not using the Facebook pixel is the worst mistake you can make as an advertiser there because it can provide you with so much valuable underlying data that it is impossible not to find a purpose for it.

How to Actually Install the Facebook Pixel

There are two ways to add the Facebook pixel to your site: manually or via a third-party plugin. I will show you both ways - each of them are good, but I recommend installing the Facebook pixel manually because it will help you not rely on plugins for this in the future. As you may know, plugins are developed by third-parties and relying solely on these means that you will add yet another "player" between you and your tracking.

How to Install the Facebook Pixel Manually

To install the Facebook pixel manually, you will first have to create the pixel using Facebook's tools. This is actually really easy:

1. Go to the Facebook Business Manager dashboard

2. Go to Ads Manager

3. Click on "Pixels"

4. Click on the green button saying "Create a Pixel"

5. Click on "Manually Install the Code Yourself"

6. You will be shown a code at this point. Copy this and paste it in a notepad to keep close by.

Next, you will have to use this code and paste it into your website's code. There are numerous ways to do this, but the single easiest one (especially for people who don't have coding experience) is to install a plugin called "Headers and Footers" in Wordpress.

Do keep in mind that if your site is not on Wordpress and you are running an eCommerce store on Shopify or you will have to manually install the code by pasting it yourself in the Header section of your site's code.

To do this, follow these steps:

1. Go to your Wordpress dashboard

2. On the left-hand side panel click "Plugins"

3. Search for "Headers and Footers"

4. Download and install the plugin

Once this is done, you can use this plugin to easily add your Facebook pixel code, following these steps:

1. Go to your notepad document and copy the Facebook pixel code

2. Go to your Wordpress dashboard

3. On the left-hand side panel click "Settings"

4. Click on "Headers and Footers" in the drop-down that will appear under "Settings"

5. Paste your Facebook pixel code in the "Settings" field

6. Click "Save"

That's it! You will have to test whether or not your Facebook pixel works, but I will show you this towards the end of this chapter.

If you want to use a third-party plugin to install your Facebook pixel, things are much easier - but do keep in mind that, as I previously said, relying on third-party apps and plugins is not always a good idea. If they go down, you go down with them (this is not to say that it will actually happen, but it is always best to be self-reliant).

That being said, if you want to proceed on this path, one of the very best and most popularly used plugins for the Facebook pixel is the Pixel Caffeine plugin, created by AdEspresso. To use it in your pixel installation process, follow these steps:

1. Go to your Wordpress dashboard

2. Click on "Plugins" on the left-hand sidebar

3. Search and Install "Pixel Caffeine"

4. A new option, "Pixel Caffeine" will appear on the left-hand sidebar in your Wordpress dashboard. Click on that

5. Click on the "General Settings" tab

6. Click on "Facebook Connect"

7. Click "OK" on the pop-up window

8. Select "Add account" and then "Pixel ID"

9. Copy your pixel ID from Facebook Ads Manager

10. Paste it in the "Pixel ID" section in Pixel Caffeine

11. Click on "Apply"

Aside from the ease of installation, the Pixel Caffeine plugin will provide you with a series of benefits:

- You can create custom audiences based on your audience's behavior on your Wordpress site right from the Wordpress dashboard

- If you have Woocommerce installed on your Wordpress (so, basically, if you run an eCommerce site from Wordpress), you can create dynamic ads right from the Wordpress dashboard

- You can track conversions so that you can see how well (or not well) your campaigns are doing.

Regardless of which method you might have chosen for your Facebook pixel installation, you will also want to make sure it *works*. Testing this is very important because you want to be absolutely certain your pixel is up and running, so that you can receive data from it into your Ads Manager and create efficient ads.

To test the installation, you will need Chrome as a browser and a Chrome extension. More specifically, follow these steps:

1. Go to https://chrome.google.com/webstore/detail/facebook-pixel-helper/fdgfkebogiimcoedlicjlajpkdmockpc?hl=en

2. Click on "Add to Chrome"

3. Go to any page of your site

4. Click on the Facebook Pixel Helper icon (right side to the search bar)

5. If pixels are active on the page, the extension will notify you of this.

Another way you can check the installation of the pixel helper is by following these steps:

1. Open a new tab with your site

2. Open a tab with Facebook Business Manager

3. Go to "Ads Manager"

4. Go to "Pixels"

5. If the Facebook pixel is active and well installed, you will see a green little dot in the top right hand of the box that will pop on the screen.

As you can see, installing and checking the installation of the Facebook pixel is really easy - and you have multiple ways of doing it. Keep in mind that this pixel is very important especially when you don't have enough followers on Facebook, or when you simply want to leverage the power of dynamic ads and coordinate them with your users' experience on your site.

In the next chapter, I will teach you how to use Facebook retargeting to your best advantage - and after that, I will dive in deeper into the more artistic part of creating Facebook ads that work (because, as you will soon learn, the *technicalities* are one thing, but the creative side is just as important).

How to Use Facebook Retargeting

Facebook retargeting is one of the most powerful digital marketing tools of the moment. There are two main reasons that make this tool so important and so successful at the same time:

- Everyone is on Facebook

- Retargeting allows you to remind people of you

Let's go back to traditional marketing and advertising for a bit, so that you can understand the true power of Facebook retargeting and why it has pushed digital marketing into a whole new age of performance.

Imagine, let's say, that you go to a really good restaurant at 8 pm, enter, but there isn't enough room inside, so you just go to another restaurant. The following week, you decide to go out with your friends at 5 pm, but can't pick a spot. In traditional marketing, the first restaurant (where you did not have enough room in the first place) wouldn't be able to remind you that they exist and that they have spare seats inside. In digital marketing (i.e. Facebook advertising), that restaurant would be able to actually reach out to you through ads (e.g. you would see an ad in your Facebook feed encouraging you to call the restaurant and book a table.

Let's take another example. You are at the mall, strolling around, and enter a clothing store to simply look around. You take a look at some clothes, you may even grab one to take to the checkout. Eventually, however, you decide that you don't want to buy anything right now, so you head to the exit. In traditional marketing and advertising, the store wouldn't be able to pop a message at the mall exit saying "Hey, are you sure you don't want this *insert item you wanted to buy*?:

In digital marketing, however, all of this is actually possible - and retargeting is precisely what you should look into if this type of campaigns interest you.

Research shows that 3 out 4 users actually notice retargeting ads[5] - and it's pretty hard not to notice that pair of shoes you've been looking at for 20 minutes is "following" you on Facebook as well.

Even more, studies also show that retargeting ads tend to be 75% more successful[6] than any other type of display ads. It is extremely easy to understand *why*, in the end: retargeted ads are all about what customers actually *want*, as opposed to what marketers think customers would want to see according to a specific set of data and demographic information.

Of course, retargeting can get annoying to customers when they feel overwhelmed with how many times you have reminded them of your products (you would feel the same if someone kept knocking on your door, trying to sell you the same product over and over again, wouldn't you?). And this is why it is important to know how to "dose" your retargeting so that you don't asphyxiate your potential customers with your offer and so that you know the right "amount" of ads you need to display to give people a little nudge.

It's all basic psychology and sociology, in the end - and I will

---

[5] Marvin, G. (2019). Survey: 3 Out Of 4 Consumers Now Notice Retargeted Ads - Marketing Land. Retrieved from https://marketingland.com/3-out-4-consumers-notice-retargeted-ads-67813

[6] 30 ways to get more Facebook Ads clicks than you ever imagined - Connectio. (2019). Retrieved from https://connectio.io/30-ways-improve-facebook-ads-ctr/

dive deeper into this in the last chapter of this book (which is coincidentally also the largest and most extensive one, precisely because the information there is genuinely important beyond all kinds of "technicalities").

OK, so Facebook Retargeting is obviously useful - but how do you properly pull it off?

The next section is dedicated to all the techniques you should use to bring Facebook Retargeting on your side and really make the absolute most out of it.

How Does Retargeting Work?

Remember the Facebook pixel, which I described in the previous chapter?

The short answer to "How does Facebook Retargeting work?" is that: the Facebook pixel. That's how and why the retargeting works and why it is so important to have the pixel installed on your site (but I have discussed this already, so I will not go into this again).

Aside from the Facebook pixel, you can also retarget people based on a list you upload to Facebook Ads Manager. This could be a list of:

- People who subscribed to your newsletter

- People who visited your physical store and agreed to be contacted for offers

- People who attended an offline or online event you held

- Specific clients from your database (who, I need to emphasize this, have agreed to have their personal information used in marketing purposes)

... And the list goes on and on.

Both the Facebook pixel and the list-based retargeting (also known as remarketing) are extremely powerful tools that will help you target the precise people who have either fallen off the funnel or got stuck somewhere on their way to conversion.

Once you have installed your pixel on your site, Facebook will allow you to track your site conversions according to:

- Custom Conversions - you can track actions users take on your site, for instance, you can track who ends on the "Thank You" page after making a purchase.

or

- Standard events - you can track different types of set events, such as:

  o Search

  o Add to cart

  o Add to wishlist

  o Add payment information

These are just some examples, as Facebook will offer you more options in this sense. Select the one that fits your particular needs the best and allow the pixel to help you target the exact groups of people you need to target.

So, the way retargeting works is by recording information about the users who do a specific action on your site and then triggering those users with the ads you want.

Simple, right?

How to Create a Retargeting Campaign on Facebook

Once your pixel is all set up and once you understand how Facebook Retargeting ads work, it's all pretty straightforward in terms of the steps you need to take to create an actual retargeting campaign. More exactly, you should circle back to what I tackled in the first chapters of this book: creating an audience (based on your website traffic this time), and then create a campaign and one (or more) ads based on this.

Here are the specific steps you need to follow:

1. Go to your Facebook Business Manager

2. Go to "Audiences"

3. Click on "Create Audience" (you will find this on the upper left-hand side of the screen)

4. Click on "Custom Audiences" in the drop-down menu

5. You will have to choose from five types of audiences:

   - Users who visit your website (general)

   - Users who visit specific pages on your site (e.g. product pages, people who reach the "Thank You" page, etc.)

   - Users who visit certain pages

   - Users who haven't visited your site in a given amount of time

   - A combination of any of the above

6. Create ad campaigns for your chosen audience.

I need to expand a bit on the last point here because it is of utmost importance that you understand a very important element of success on Facebook ads: technicalities and the way you actually target customers are one thing, but you still need great campaigns to make this work for you.

Your ads need to match your audience not only from the point of view of who they are displayed to but from the point of view of the message behind you. The second half of this book is dedicated entirely to understanding how advertising works and how people relate to it - precisely because it is really, really crucial that you don't just pour money in displaying mediocre ads to people who might otherwise be genuinely interested in them.

No matter how great you are at targeting and how in-depth you know the intricacies of Facebook ads and the options the platform offers, it still comes down to good advertising. Otherwise, your ads will be ignored at the very best and downright annoying at the very worst (creating the exact opposite effect of what you want them to).

The Science and Art of Creating a Facebook Ad Campaign

Digital marketing is a spectacular field to be in - and one you should actually be in regardless of what business you run. You may be a local seamstress or you may be the biggest soda company in the world - digital marketing can still provide you with tremendous benefits that will push your business forward.

Digital marketing is amazing because it lies at the confluence between science and art, between the old and the new, between pure technicality and true creativity.

In many ways, digital marketing is just plain and simply marketing brought to the digital age - or more specifically, marketing that uses digital channels as a means of sending messages.

The first half of this book has been dedicated to showing you how Facebook ads work: why they are so popular, how to create custom and lookalike audiences, how to set up campaigns and ads, how to understand the marketing objective behind them, how to make the most out of the Facebook pixel, and, finally, how to use Facebook Retargeting to the best of your advantage.

The second half of this book is dedicated to helping you understand why some ads and marketing campaigns are successful and others are, well, not that successful. Beyond all the settings on Facebook ads and beyond the magnificent ways you can narrow down your audience, your message is what makes the people *click*.

And great messages start with the basic understanding of what advertising and marketing are, where they come from, and how to use them in an efficient way - rather than tossing them around on a game of chance.

There's no such thing as bad advertising, they say. Most of the times, this is related to how Hollywood stars' scandals boost their popularity. But I'm going to use this with an entirely different meaning: ads don't work because somewhere along the way, you took the wrong decision - not because your audience doesn't respond to ads or because your business isn't advertisable.

Not taking the wrong decision lies, in the end, in knowledge and understanding - knowledge of what the fundamental marketing concepts are and understanding of how to "tickle" your audience in a way that makes them do what you want them to do.

So, let's dive in.

What Is Marketing? What Is Advertising? Are They Different?

Marketing and advertising seem like two terms that are gratuitously tossed around like there's no tomorrow.

Market yourself.

The best product on the market.

Let's do some marketing for our store.

These are phrases you have definitely heard a thousand and one times before - but the sad reality is that most people don't actually understand what *marketing* or *advertising* is.

They are something related to image and promotions, but most people's understanding of both these concepts is either limited or completely misled. That's understandable, though: the more these terms get tossed around, the more people feel they are familiar with them and that they know everything there is to know about them.

Let me tell you something, though: nobody knows everything about marketing and advertising and nobody can promise you 100% success with a given recipe. If you ever see any kind of marketing or advertising service advertised as a 100% guarantee, turn around and run like you're running for your own life, because it's most certainly a scam.

Going back to what marketing and advertising actually are, people aren't very far from the truth: these are, indeed, both related to image and promotions. But the intricacies of both marketing and advertising go far deeper than that - they go deep into understanding the human being and what triggers people, they go deep into psychology and sociology, they go deep into literature and wording, as well as art itself.

So, what is marketing?

Put in basic terms, marketing is about promoting products or services, but it is also about creating meaningful relationships with your potential customers. In fact, before you even think of *selling*, you should think of your customers and what they want and need - that's where true success in this field will be found.

What is advertising?

One mistake a lot of people make is overlapping marketing and advertising as nearly synonymous terms. However, there is a pretty big distinction between the two. Namely, advertising is defined as a *type* of marketing communication that is openly sponsored.

So, marketing is the tree, and advertising is a branch of it.

Marketing is about creating the need on the market, about educating the customers, about bringing them closer to the company through various means - and advertising is about selling to customers by using a combination of artistic devices and sales techniques.

Marketing is about statistics, it is about targeting, it is about the way produce in a supermarket is arranged on the shelves, it is about t-shirts, it is about employment branding, it is about a thousand and one things, all at once.

Advertising is but a slice of the marketing cake - it is straightforward promotion of a product. Everyone knows an ad when they see it: and that is because of the structure, the placement, and the very nature of an ad point to itself.

Not everyone knows marketing when they see it, though. For instance, if you create a marketing campaign to loyalize people to a certain brand of apples sold by a certain company, you might want to release a free book on recipes that include those specific apples.

Of course, this is one example - and a simplistic one, at that.

What other types of marketing communications are there, aside from advertising? Well, here are some:

- Direct Marketing (think of Avon catalogs)

- Personal selling (think of door-to-door salesmen demonstrating products to sell them)

- Public relations (think of the statements released by big companies, such as the statement released by Volkswagen in the wake of their scandal a couple of years ago)

- Sponsorship (think of the clothes worn by tennis players)

In digital marketing, advertising and marketing are frequently intertwined tighter than in traditional marketing - but there still is a pretty big difference between them.

In general, digital marketers refer to *marketing* as everything that produces organic results (e.g. a blog post that is optimized for Search Engine Optimization).

Digital marketers also refer to *advertising* as everything that produces paid results (e.g. Facebook Ads, Google AdWords, etc.).

Yes, marketing and advertising are different. But maybe more than anything, they are frequently misunderstood.

To many people (including many executives), a digital marketer is a person who posts *stuff* on Facebook - and not because there's an actual goal to this, but because every other business does it.

Digital marketing (and, more specifically to this book, Facebook marketing) goes way beyond that.

It goes into granularly targeting customers and helping them move further into the sales funnel.

It goes into getting to know your customers at a personal level without investing thousands (and even tens, hundreds of thousands) of hard-earned dollars in market research.

It goes into making advertising accessible for all businesses, small and large alike.

Digital marketing is democratic at its very core: everyone can do it, and everyone can do it well, provided that the basics of marketing *and* digitalization are well-covered in terms of knowledge.

Yes, you *can* do digital marketing on your own. But it isn't as simple as posting a couple of kitten photos on Facebook.

Traditional Marketing vs. Online Marketing

Marketing has been around since the very first exchange of products.

Sure, they didn't call it marketing back then - but it was there. Homosapiens No. 1 sold fur, and Homosapiens No. 2 sold tools. They both needed each other and they both knew that - so they exchanged products according to the value of those products and according to what the market offered (e.g. furs might have been harder to procure than tools, and tools are needed to procure fur).

I went a long way back there, but if you want to think of a better example, think of marketing as, well, a *physical market where people sell and buy things.* For better exemplifying, imagine a typical Middle-East or Indian market, where negotiation is always part of the experience. Everyone there sets up their market tables nicely to showcase the best of the best products, and everyone there tries to attract buyers to their table.

Once there, the negotiation begins - and there's a true art to that. On the one hand, the seller wants to sell the product with the highest price they can. On the other hand, they also want to give the buyer the satisfaction of a bargain. To do that, the seller must have a very good understanding of how human psychology works. Sure, market sellers might not have a very in-depth theoretical understanding of all of this - but even so, they have the innate ability to convince you that:

- Their products are the best

- Their prices are the best

- You can do a lot with their products

- You are winning because you get the best product, for the best price, with the best use.

The same basic principles apply in everything sold, everywhere in the world. As a marketer, you need to make your audience feel that they have the upper hand - the decision is in their hands. You are just providing them with the facts that will make them buy from you, as opposed to the other market table.

Coming closer to the topic of this section, traditional marketing is all about the means by which a product or service is marketed. This ranges from product placement in movies to paper magazine articles explaining the use of a service or products, t-shirts, branded merchandise for clients, promotional contests, and so on.

Traditional marketing isn't that much different than online marketing - it's just that it is frequently more expensive and not many small companies dab into it. Why? Because it is expensive and it can frequently show little for all the investment. It's not that traditional marketing doesn't yield results - it does. But the sad truth is that they are quite difficult to track.

Just think of Coca-Cola. When you run a campaign offering free branded glasses for every two bottles of Coke, can you actually track how many people continued to buy Coca-Cola as a clear result of this campaign?

Well, not really. You can run expensive market research studies and ask people about this, but the path of the customer from the glass to the glass filled with Coca-Cola is hard to determine. It's more guesswork than data - and for a very expensive price, at that.

In digital marketing, however, technology makes it all easier.

You can actually track the people who come to your site, the people who continue their journey down the funnel, the people who are retained, and even the people who promote your products to other people. And you don't have to break the bank to do that - most of this data can be acquired with Google Analytics and a couple of other tools that will help you narrow down your data and pinpoint the moment people convert.

In digital marketing, you can actually re-contact the people who ordered a set of new nice glasses. And you can walk them on the path to buying the soda as well.

So, the major difference between traditional and online marketing lies in more than just the channels of communication: it lies in the way you actually track down your results as well, it lies in the investment you make in your campaigns, it lies in the nature of the architecture you build around of a campaign.

At this point, you might be tempted to think that traditional marketing and digital marketing are as far from each other as a sunny day of summer is from a snowy night of winter.

That's not entirely true, though.

Both traditional and online marketing is based on the same foundation: communication, knowing your audience and tapping into their needs and desires.

Ironically, this is where most marketers (even experienced ones!) make the first major faux pas. They focus so much on the technicalities of their campaigns, targeting, pixels, and everything in between that they forget the essentials: that your campaigns need to target actual people, not robots that automatically fit into your selected criteria and automatically buy from you because they displayed an ad.

Beyond pixels and targeting and audience selection, you should always keep in mind that you are initiating a channel of communication with *people*. People who have dreams, aspirations, desires, emotions. People who might or might not have families. Who might like cats, or dogs, or both. People who drink coffee in the morning and people who work extra hard to pay rent next month.

Real people, with real issues you can offer a solution to.

All marketing communication, online and offline, is narrowed down to a very simple theory: that of the communication channel. No matter who you are and who your partner of communication is, there will always be five basic elements to consider:

- The sender of the message

- The channel used to send the message

- The language used to send the message (which, keep in mind, can be *articulated* or not)

- The noise (the interference you might encounter between you and your receiver)

- The receiver

The same basic components apply to *all* communication. Let's take two examples, as far away from each other as possible, to demonstrate this.

Let's say you want to meet with your best friend for drinks tonight. You are the sender of a message in this situation, right? You call them to ask them out (and the "phone line" becomes your channel). You use plain English language to send your message - but because this is your best friend, your English is not formal at all. Hell, you might even toss a few curses in between (because that's what besties do, right?). Because you are walking down the street, there's a lot of noise around you (it's midday and everyone's buzzing around). So, to make sure your friend hears you, you enter a street enclave that seems quieter. Of course, you know your message receiver very well (you went to kindergarten together), so even if they're not very convinced that they should go out today, you can win them on your side with arguments you *know for sure* will work on them.

And now let's extrapolate the same concepts to an example that's very different. Let's say you are a marketer for a company selling agricultural technology. You are the sender of the message and you want to convince your receiver (a mid-sized farmer) that your tractors are the best option there is. To do this, you will post an article on a website niched on mid-sized farmers. You will use plain English to send your message across - but because this is B2B communication, you will use a more formal approach. Even more, you will toss in specific terms connected to agriculture too (because you need to speak in the same "slang" as your audience does). You want to make sure your message gets across loud and clear, so you will be very straightforward in the way you craft and structure your article, not leaving room for confusion in any way. Because you are a marketer and you have studied your audience's behavior, as well as your competition's marketing techniques and products, you will use arguments that are *likely* to win the target audience on your side.

As you can see, all communication relies on the same basic scheme - the key is knowing which elements to adapt and how, so that your message gets across and convinces/ engages.

Both traditional and online marketing is about people more than anything. The means by which your message gets across (organically or not) are just that: means. The message, however, is where you will find the true secret of success in marketing and advertising.

It's not something anyone can teach you step by step. It's not something you can learn in class. It's not something you can apply a given recipe for and know for certain that you will win.

In traditional marketing, your odds of winning new customers (and proving that you did that) are foggy.

In online marketing, you are given with all the tools you need to clear the air out and create a clean channel of communication between you and your future customers.

Going back to the tree analogy, if marketing is the tree and advertising is a branch, then online and offline marketing are two mirroring halves of the same tree crown. On the one traditional marketing side, the leaves are green and the crown is rich and old. But on the online marketing side, the leaves are green and you can actually see, *live*, how the flowers of the tree are blooming from in between the trees.

OK, so why all the talk about marketing if this book is all about advertising?

Because without proper marketing knowledge, you will not be able to pull off ads that work. I know it might not seem so when you watch Mad Men - but do keep in mind those were different times and, more importantly, that's a fictional show that reveals only a very small part of how advertising actually works.

To make your advertising campaigns successful, you need to know the differences between online and offline communication - as well as what brings them together at their very core. To make your ads work, you need to know your channel, your audience, your message, and the potential interferences between you and your receiver.

Owned vs. Paid Content Online and Offline

Alright, so you now understand the basic difference and the fundamental resemblance between traditional and digital marketing.

Both "traditional marketing" and "digital marketing" are, most likely, terms you have stumbled upon before.

What about "owned" media vs "paid media"?

Well, that's another distinction I feel we must make for a better understanding of how (and when) successful Facebook ads happened.

Basically, owned content/media and paid content/media are exactly that: content/media you own, as opposed to content/media you pay for.

Let me give you some examples to help you understand this better.

Owned content is what you post on your website's blog. You have paid for the domain, you own copyright on it, and you own everything on it.

Paid content is what you post on a Facebook ad promoting your blog.

Owned media is defined by any kind of property you have on the web which you can control 100% and which is absolutely unique to your particular brand. Your social media channels (your actual Facebook page, for example) and your website, as well as anything that is tied into your website (a landing page for example or a case study that circles back to your site and your products/services). In traditional marketing, owned media would be the posters and banners, the magazine your company publishes, and so on.

Owned media can be promoted in various ways - such as by optimizing it for search engines (on-page and SEO), by linking back to it from other websites related to your niche (off-page SEO), or by paying for promotions.

It is important to own your own media/content because this is something nobody can take away from you. Plus, it's something that is intrinsically tied into your very brand - something that will help you create an image, educate your audience, and ultimately, convert them into actual buyers/ users.

Paid media, on the other hand, is not something you own per se. It is, most of the time, a good way to promote content you already own. Do keep in mind that while paying to promote your content is definitely a great way to attract some traffic, it should not be the only thing you rely on when it comes to your marketing approach - that means you will endlessly pour money into bringing people on your site, as opposed to attracting some of them to get the ball rolling and make them engage with your content to ultimately generate actual sales.

Online, there are two major categories of paid media sources: social media advertising and Google advertising. Of course, some sites might sell their own space for online advertising and sponsored articles, but the vast majority of businesses turn to social media and Google advertising when they want to pay for promotions.

Offline, paid media is all advertising you see on TV, on the side of the street, in newspapers and magazines, on the radio, and so on. How much you pay for these depends on how watched/how public/how well-read a particular medium is, as well as the placement of the ad, and its length/ size.

Somewhere beyond paid and owned content/media, there's also something called "earned media". This is a way of promotion you *earn* as opposed to *paying for*. In other words, this is evangelism for content. When you create excellent content and people like it, they will very likely share it with their peers. Viral content is earned content at its very finest and at its very highest - but that is difficult to achieve and the sad truth is that there's no actual recipe for it (as I mentioned before, there's no given recipe for anything related to digital marketing).

In traditional marketing, earned media is *the word of mouth* - when you recommend a product or a by-product to someone else because you actually believe in it. You have bought it, you have tested it, you loved it, and you want everyone you know to use it because it's *that* good.

So, where should you place most of your efforts when doing digital marketing?

Everywhere.

No, really, everywhere. The best way to tackle digital marketing and actually win customers with it is by combining owned, paid, and earned content. In today's landscape, you can't really have one without another. It used to be that organic reach was enough, true - but with algorithms changing (especially on social media), reaching your target audience organically has grown to be quite difficult without a bit of a push.

And that's one important role of social media advertising - it can help you get the ball rolling and gain some traction for your content.

DO note, however, that it is not the only role and that social media ads can go beyond promoting your traffic. As already shown in this book, you can use social media to actually nudge people farther down the sales funnel.

Content Marketing That Works

While this book was entirely dedicated to paid media (namely, Facebook ads), I feel that it is extremely important to talk about content marketing for a bit too.

The reason I choose to include this in this book is that people need to understand that paid advertising can't work miracles. It can definitely help you convert people, it can help you boost your content's reach, and it can even help you draw important conclusions about your buyer persona.

What paid advertising can rarely do, however, is make people feel safe with your business. It doesn't matter if you sell bread or cybersecurity products - ads are not necessarily how you make users trust your business. There's some sort of innate rejection of people when it comes to advertising - it can convince them to buy, but a trustworthiness dimension needs to be added to the mix.

Even more, paid advertising cannot create loyal customers. It can nudge them into buying again, but it takes a bit more to build a loyal customer base.

Paid advertising cannot inform customers. It can put the information in front of their eyes, but it cannot actually inform them - precisely because it is frequently perceived as untrustworthy.

Paid advertising cannot create actual evangelism - it can nudge it, but it can't actually push people into sharing your content and believing in it.

Does that mean paid advertising is *bad*?

No, at all - I have relaid some of the essential benefits behind paid advertising (on Facebook, in this case) all throughout the book.

But it is extremely important to acknowledge that content marketing should be part of your marketing strategy if you want more than one-off sales. Content marketing is where the magic of the relationship between buyer and seller happens - where the connection is built, and where retention begins.

How to make content marketing work?

Here are some basic tips that will help you with this:

1. It must be quality. I know you have heard "Content is king" at least a million times before, but the truth is that it keeps being repeated for one simple reason: it works, it can make all the difference in the world, and it should lie at the very core of your entire marketing strategy precisely because it ads *soul* to your marketing.

2. It must be diverse. It used to be that written content was king. But these days, it's more of a mixture that leans towards video content. People love images and they love watching videos - so this is something you should actually invest time and resources in. Otherwise, you are missing out on a crucially important channel that is continuously growing in terms of popularity.

Aside from video content, you must also make sure to create other types of content suitable for your target audiences. For instance, if you sell to other businesses, case studies tend to work very well. If you sell to consumers, you might want to create content that helps them incorporate your products in real life (e.g. if you sell shoes, you could create a stylebook to help people inspire their new outfits with shoes from your store).

Infographics, charts, articles, videos, slideshows, and everything in between - it is all content. The key lies in making sure your content is diverse precisely because this is a very important way to spread it across multiple channels and reach a higher audience.

3. It must be optimized. It doesn't matter where you post your content: it absolutely has to be optimized for searches. Every search engine has its own rules as to how you can reach the top of their results pages - however, the basics are pretty much all the same everywhere: you need some keywords with a high reach and low competition. You need to use them organically in your content and in the description of your content, you need to have a mobile-friendly channel, and you should create the entire content with latent-semantic indexing in mind (i.e. using LSI keywords that are semantically related to your main one).

4. It must look good. Look what, people love visuals. That's why Instagram is really popular, that's why people spend hours and hours every day on Facebook and YouTube. We're visual creatures - our brains are actually wired to pay more attention to images and retain information better when we *watch* something, as opposed to *reading* it. This is an actual fact - and you need to use it in your content strategy. Yes, that includes the blog articles as well - they need to look good (i.e. to be structured in a way that allows users to skim and scan the text) and they need to be associated with good graphics and pictures (really high quality, not shaky-phone-photo-quality).

5. It must engage. There's no point in creating content if you don't want it to start an actual conversation of some

sort - directly with you/your company or among users. Engaging content is how earned media is, well, *earned*. You might not always be able to control what people comment on and whether they do it or not - because sometimes, people just share thoughts in private as opposed to posting them for everyone to see. However, what you can do is set your content up for engagement: using "you", asking questions, using a tone that connects to the user, and so on.

6. It must have the target audience at its core. I cannot emphasize how important this is. It happens very frequently that marketing communication professionals create content that fits the business, but doesn't fit the audience - and that's truly the worst mistake you can ever make.

Just think of it: you don't want to engage your workmates (unless you are creating internal marketing materials, which is an entirely different deal). You want to engage potential buyers (or at least people that might influence potential buyers). Your content has to address that audience - it needs to be crafted in a way that puts them at the very core of your entire content strategy.

Without this, your content is just plain and simply useless - and no amount of paid advertising can ever bring in the stream of constant content consumers you need to create a brand, a reputation, a true connection with your (potential) buyers.

7. It must be unique. Everything that could have been said on the internet has already been said. Unless your content focuses on very current news (e.g. new algorithm updates from Google), you need to find a true voice and a true sense of uniqueness to your content.

Yes, you can technically create SEO content that will attract people to your page. And yes, your content can be, at least in theory, purely technical: it can offer the information in a clean and pretty way.

Beyond all that, however, your content needs to have your own voice in it. It needs to speak. It needs to stand out in the way the message is packaged and delivered.

Think out of the box - it is, indeed, the only thing you can do in a world overflood by lifeless content.

8. It must be evergreen. That means that the content you post today should stand just as valid tomorrow, one month from now, and four years from now too. This kind of content brings in a constant stream of consumers - and when they come to your site (or wherever your content is published), they will continue to find value in your content regardless of how long it's been since it was originally posted there.

9. It must attract. This is mostly related to the headlines you associate with your content, as well as with a point already covered above: uniqueness. People are bombarded with tons of content every single day, every single second they spend on the internet - and the first thing they see when they stumble upon something is your headlines. Create awesome headlines - the kind that really make people click. Sure, they need to be SEO-friendly - but they need to instill curiosity in your readers too (which circles us back to the concept according to which all content is to be created with the target audience as its main guiding star).

10. It must be consistent. This has two ramifications: your content must be consistent in the way it is posted (i.e. it

should be regularly uploaded) and your content must follow the same style all the time. To make sure this happens no matter how many freelancers or employees work on your content, creating a style guide is really important.

11. It must be scheduled. It can be really hard to keep up with posting regular content when you are busy with a thousand other things. However, please do note that your content can be scheduled ahead. A content calendar can be a true lifesaver because it will allow you to have a constant stream of content posted on your main channels.

12. It must be repurposed. Want to make the most out of the long hours you worked on that amazing article? Repurpose it: create videos, infographics, presentations out of it. This will allow you to squeeze as much juice as you can from every piece of content you ever publish for your company.

13. It must be updated. If anything has changed since you posted your content for the first time, do make sure to update it. For instance, an article about Facebook ads in 2015 will not offer the same information as an article about Facebook ads in 2019 - it will probably need some severe updates. Don't have old content just sitting around - bring it back to life by updating it to the freshest news on the market.

14. It must be promoted. Ads are one way to do it - we have already established that. Another way to promote your content is by posting guest posts. This comes with a double-benefit: it will improve your SEO and it will link back to the best pieces of content you have published as well.

Another way to promote your content is by asking questions on Quora that are connected to it. For example, if you have posted an article about Facebook ads, you can search the topic on Quora and help people find answers by providing it to them and linking back to your own extended piece on that particular topic.

15. It must be adapted to the buyer's journey down the funnel. Someone who has never heard of your business will read a completely different article than someone who has bought from you before. The key to coordinating your content marketing efforts with your sales is making sure you create content that fits the stage at which your customers are in their funnel journey.

This might take some time to figure out, especially when you have no idea where to start out. However, it is the key to opening a treasure trove of value for your content.

16. It must be tracked. Your content marketing is not about the likes and shares you get. It's about the value it creates. Tracking your content is not about the number of people who land on your pages either - it is about that just as much as it is about the amount of time people spend with your content and where it leads them.

My suggestion is using Google Analytics Goals to track the performance of your content in relation to the buyer's journey in the sales funnel. Doing this will help you adjust your content correctly so that you can see even more results yielded from your work.

Of course, these are just the absolute basics of content marketing that work. Same as with paid advertising, entire libraries could be written about this topic -- and it still wouldn't be covered in its entirety, precisely because there will always be changes in how content is done, tracked, and consumed.

Content marketing is not a fast-and-easy element of your digital marketing strategy. It's an element that takes time to build - and in most cases, it also takes time to see results from as well.

Why is content marketing important to Facebook ads?

Because the two of them are connected - you can't have excellent ad ROI if you don't have good content to back it up, and, as of lately, you can't have excellent performance on your content without investing a bit in its promotion as well.

Content marketing and Facebook ads can go hand in hand - and they should both be coordinated with the basic principles of marketing communication I will relay a bit later on (and which have been touched upon before in the book as well).

Where Advertising Falls in the Digital Marketing Landscape

Advertising has a tendency to polarize people - particularly people working behind the ads, but people who are targeted by these ads as well.

On the one hand, you have digital marketers who swear by paid ads and say that they are the golden pot at the end of the rainbow.

On the other hand, you have digital marketers who barely invest in paid ads because they either don't see the value in it or because they have not incorporated paid ads in a cohesive, well-coordinated marketing strategy (and thus, they only see this as a waste of time and money).

And on the other side of the fence, you have people who are actually passionate about advertising, people who don't mind it, people who make use of it, and people who are downright pissed off by it.

Unless your target audience falls 100% in that last category, you will still find a role for your paid campaign to play in your overall marketing strategy.

Advertising is not evil, it is not a waste of financial resources and time, and it is not the recipe to fabricating gold either.

It's somewhere in between: and whether it leans towards one end of the spectrum or the other is all about the way you build your advertising campaigns and the way you incorporate it with your overall marketing and business approach.

If you have tried Facebook ads before and failed, it isn't

because Facebook ads are inherently bad - it is because you most likely did not understand *how* to create ads that are successful. Hopefully, this book will have solved this issue for you with all the information provided in it.

So, where does advertising lie in the entire digital marketing space?

Well, advertising in the digital marketing paradigm is like the push you need to jump off a plane when you do skydiving,

It is also like that fancy, expensively-dressed friend that doesn't quite fit in your friend group - but you always hang out because deep inside, you know you come from the same places.

Advertising is crucial to your digital marketing success, especially in 2019. As more and more businesses start creating content, and as more and more businesses pop up online in every niche under the Sun, you are competing with so much more than what you used to compete against just a few years ago!

Advertising can make the difference between a marketing strategy that works in theory and a marketing strategy that works in practice.

Is paid advertising, and more specifically, Facebook advertising, expensive?

Well, yes. And no, at the same time.

It can be clearly more expensive than content marketing.

But it can be adjusted to fit your budget and your expectations too. If you have $100 to spend on ads, spend them wisely on ads that are well crafted and well targeted. If you have $100,000, follow the same ground rules. In both cases, you should set your expectations straight from the very beginning: you cannot expect to turn your world upside down on $100, and you cannot expect every single cent of your $100,000 to triple in value in terms of the clients it brings in.

Advertising lies right there, in the middle of the digital marketing strategy, precisely because it helps you connect the dots: the dots between sales and marketing, the dots between content and promotion, the dots between a client who has landed on your site looking for answers and a client that ends up buying from you (once, twice, a thousand times).

It cannot be said advertising is more important than organic marketing - or the other way around.

It can just be said that they are pieces of a puzzle that cannot harmoniously come together without, well, actual harmony.

Would you diss a piece of a puzzle game because everyone's telling you to do so? Well, you could - but that would create an image with an actual hole in it. And it goes the same with advertising in digital marketing as well: without the first, the latter is an image that is pure and simply not complete.

Defining and Understanding Your Audience

Your target audience is, as I was mentioning in the Content Marketing section, at the very core of your marketing strategy.

This is where it all begins: the people you want to talk to. The people you want to send your products. The people at the other end of the communication string.

Some of you may be tempted to believe that defining a clear target audience means restricting your marketing to just a handful few of people - and thus, restricting future income for your company.

However, that is completely untrue. Targeting everyone (even if it's just everyone in a geographical area) will merely bring a few customers (even none) towards your company. The reason this happens is simple to understand: the larger your audience is, the broader your message is. And the broader your message is, the more it says little to nothing. The less your message says, the more likely it is that people will not even bother with it (not to mention not buy from you).

Spam email can be considered a form of very broad message. When you get emails about diet pills and you've never once been interested in the topic, you will pay zero interest in what that email has to say. OK, in this example, you also know that's a spam email and that it most probably contains some sort of virus too - but for the purpose of the example, let's assume viruses do not exist. Even if it's the cleanest email on Earth and even if there is zero chance it contains any kind of malevolent links or files in it, that email will just not stir any interest in you.

Suppose you *are* interested in weight loss and you actually googled the Keto Diet a couple of days ago, and then forgot about it entirely. How would you feel about an ad displayed in your Facebook Feed, saying "Hey, still confused? This will make it easy"?

You would probably be tempted to click (at the very least) or actually click right away (at the very most) - and thus, the purpose of that ad would be attained.

The difference between the two examples lies precisely in that: in understanding who your audience is and what they are looking for.

And in order to understand your audience, you must first define them.

To define your target audience, you can go two ways:

1. You can look at your current customer base and draw some conclusions from there. This can be easily done in Google Analytics, but if you want to go even further, you can run in-depth surveys on them to find out even more about their motivations and behaviors.

2. You can imagine the target audience by making assumptions based on what your product is, what it solves, and who is most likely to buy it.

DO keep in mind that this second option is much less data-based and more intuition-based, so you might have to come back to it and refine it. Most times, people use this approach when they are just starting out on a business and their customer base is not large enough to provide them with actual data on who the buyers are. However, once your customer base grows, you can always come back to your assumed target audience and fine-tune it with the data you have acquired.

Most times, marketers use a concept called "buyer persona" when talking about their target audience. A business can have one, two, or multiple buyer personas, depending on how many people they target and how those people can be categorized and projected.

The term "buyer persona" is frequently used to describe an exponent of a business' target audience - it is a term that is in itself defined as "an example of a person targeted by a company".

I highly, highly suggest that you create a buyer persona or at least a strategic messaging map before you dive into Facebook advertising. This will help you:

- Create audiences that work for your ads and business

- Create messages that are actually engaging

- Make it easier to explain to your team how your entire social media strategy will be developed

A buyer persona is someone very specific - it's an imaginary person that has a series of attributes you will construct based on who you want to target. Some of the elements included in the construction of a buyer persona include:

- A name

- Age

- Location

- Occupation

- Career stage

- Income

- Education

- General interests and hobbies

- Marital status

- Ethnicity

- Nationality

- Gender

...And so on.

You can be as specific as you want with the creation of your buyer persona. The main takeaway here is that your buyer persona should be very specific.

Once you have defined the basic features of your target audience, do make sure you ask yourself the following questions:

- Are there enough people in your target audience? Even if you have a niche product, you still want to make sure you will be able to sell enough of it to actually be able to consistently run your business.

- Will your target audience see your product as beneficial? Will they *need* or *desire* it in any way? This is really important because it lies at the foundation of your future marketing communication (including Facebook ads).

- What drives them to make decisions? For instance, some people might be more inclined to be driven by bargain offers than others - therefore, you could create campaigns that tap into that.

- Can your target audience afford your products? For example, you wouldn't want to sell luxury products to an audience whose income is on the lower side of the spectrum.

- Can you actually reach your target audience? Some people might not be on Facebook (believe it or not), so it is important to think of the methods by which you can reach them as your target audience. For instance, if your target audience mostly consists of men in the 55-75 age span who work in agriculture and live in rural areas, there is a pretty high chance that the vast majority of them will not use Facebook - and thus, you will have to find other means by which you can make your message reach them.

Let's take an example. You run an eCommerce that sells shoes, and your buyer persona is Sally. Sally is 31, she lives in New York, she has an average income of $50,000/year, and she is a digital marketer at the beginning of her road. She has higher education (a BA in Communications and Marketing), she loves cats, Netflix, and the poetry of Edgar Allan Poe, she is not married (and she is not even dating anyone at the moment), she is Caucasian and Asian, she is American, and she identifies herself as a woman.

To target Sally in a Facebook ad, you could use any of the information that define her as a buyer persona. You could create messages suitable for her age, or messages that trigger the place she lives in. You could trigger her by talking about cats or the poetry of Poe. You could trigger her by talking about the fact that her income might not be as high as she wants it to be and your products can help her save money.

Using Facebook ads, you could also create a targeting audience that Sally would fit in, both from the point of the demographic factors that make her who she is and from the point of view of the interests (you may even toss in some cat breeds and specific Netflix series she might be interested in).

Your Facebook ads (and marketing in general) should use the information you have about your buyer persona to create messages that respond to your target audience's needs and desires (I will cover how to determine these in the next section of this chapter).

Facebook is, without doubt, a tremendously powerful tool for marketers and advertisers. However advanced this tool may be, it still cannot actually *work for you*. There are some things that should happen in the background to define the future campaigns and which parts of the Facebook ads tool you will use - and one of the first such things to happen is the definition of your target audience.

DO take your time with this and DO accept the fact that you might not get it right from the very beginning. You can't know 100% who is on the other end of the communication channel when it comes to online communication (and marketing communication in general). You can only aggregate data and imagine your target audience based on that (or, in case you don't have enough data, you can just plain and simply *guess*).

Defining your target audience could make or break your entire strategy - and yet, it's something a lot of people simply glance through, not giving it the importance it deserves.

The Psychology behind Marketing

Marketing is a fascinating field lying at the confluence between economics, psychology, sociology, technology (specifically in the digital marketing sector), and art.

To be a great advertiser, you must first be a great marketer. And to be a great marketer and advertiser, you must have the basic psychology, sociology, and economy knowledge to bring technology and art on your side so that you can convince your target audience.

I want to dive in a little deeper into what the psychology of marketing actually refers to and how you can dissect your marketing goals to translate them into actions on the side of your target audience.

Put simply, the psychology behind marketing is heavily reliant on two main theories: Maslow's Pyramid of Needs and Aristotle's Causes for Human Action.

I will start with the first since it is also one of the most well-known theories and it is very likely that you have stumbled upon it in the past as well.

1. The Pyramid of Needs created by Maslow. This theory relies on the idea that there are five groups of human needs, grouped according to the importance they play in human life, and ranked from the most basic and primitive ones to the most elevated ones, as follows:

- Physiological needs - like water, food, sleeping, breathing, digestion, and so on

- Safety needs - employment, health, and so on

- Love and belonging needs - sexual intimacy, family, friendship, and so on

- Esteem needs - like self-confidence or the respect of others, for example

- Self-actualization needs - such as creativity, morality, spontaneity, etc.

Why is this pyramid of needs so important for you as a marketer or advertiser?

Basically, because it will help you understand what people want from you, even when you don't know them in person - because every single human on Earth will aspire to fulfill these needs, at least at one level or another. The higher on the Maslow's pyramid a need may be, the harder it will be to convince people of your product - precisely because those needs cannot be fulfilled physically, with palpable products.

It is not impossible, though - and the huge number of inspirational products in the self-help department of every book store prove that people truly are searching to fulfill a very specific set of needs located around the higher end of the Maslow pyramid.

Depending on what products or services you may be selling, you will have to localize your offering in one (or more) of the needs and desire groups as they have been described by Maslow. Tapping into these needs with a well-crafted message will help you convince your audience that they actually want (and need) your products - regardless of whether those products are connected to having more spare time (such as an organizational tool that taps into the self-actualization center of the pyramid) or simply eating better food (such as a healthy type of cereal that taps into both the primary physiological needs and the health ones).

1. Aristotle's causes for human action. Surprisingly for many, the very basics of persuasion go as far back as Ancient Greece - and one of the forefathers in this specific slice of philosophy is none other than Aristotle.

According to him, humans action is sourced in seven causes:

- Chance. To take action, every human has to have the chance to do it. For example, most people will most likely give in to a super-discount if they are offered the chance to do so.

- Nature. A lot of actions are caused by none other than human nature. For example, if everyone in your group of friends and relatives owns a smartphone of any kind, you will eventually end up wanting one as well. Of course, this is quite an "advanced" example, as human nature can be the cause of purchases that are considered to be much less luxurious than a smartphone.

- Compulsion. Ever wondered why the space leading up to the cash register is lined up with all sorts of random items - from condoms to chewing gum, candy bars, and mini flashlights? It is because years and years of studies and experience have taught marketers and salespeople that, while waiting in line to be cashed in, people are very likely to give into compulsion and buy things they don't necessarily need *right now* - like chewing gum or another bar of chocolate. These, my dear reader, are compulsion-based buys - and if your products are suitable for this kind of purchase, you should definitely create campaigns that *urge* people to buy, rather than convince them.

- Habit. A lot of marketers and advertisers forgo this, focusing on attracting large chunks of (potential) customers into the sales funnel. However, the truth is that enticing people to use your product can actually bring in more cash for your company. For instance, if you sell cereal and you loyalize your audience, they will come to buy the same kind of cereal for weeks, months, years, and even decades in a row.

- Reason. Some actions are caused by nothing more than just plain and simple reason. When you need a new pair of running shoes because the old ones are worn out, you buy them. When your dishwasher is broken beyond repair, you buy a new one - and more importantly, you study the market to make the best decision for your budget and needs. Reason is the underlying cause for many purchases - and the way to tap into this is by providing factual evidence of your product helping people (studies, comparisons, and so on).

- Passion. Although it's definitely not recommended for buyers, a lot of actions are triggered by emotions and passions. Sometimes, it may happen for small products - such as a pair of jeans advertised to slim down the body. Other times, it may happen for larger products - such as cars that are advertised to make a life change (or simply whose brand is built around that). It is fair to say that no matter the nature of your product, tapping into the emotions your target audience might be experiencing will help you sell more - because, in the end, your product should be offering a solution to a need (as described in the previous paragraphs, focusing on Maslow's pyramid of needs). And when you learn how to tap into the emotional needs of people, you have struck gold!

- Desire. Some actions and purchases are triggered by

desire. You want a new iPhone not because the old one is broken or because it can't be used anymore - you want it because it's new, shiny, and it is associated with certain brand values you want to project out into the world. Other, less expensive, and equally efficient products might exist - but none can be as well-regarded as an Apple product, especially when your entire circle of friends and relatives owns one.

Aside from Maslow's Pyramid of Needs and the Seven Causes of the Human Action as seen by Aristotle, you will also have to keep in mind some basics on how *persuasion* itself works. Why?

Because knowing what moves people is one thing - but actually moving them is a completely different thing.

According to Vance Packard, a journalist and social critic who was active in the '50s and '60s, persuasion is based on three major pillars: reciprocity, scarcity, and emotional appeal.

You'd think that *"Yeah, but that was a billion years ago"*, but the absolute truth is that the same basics are applied today as well, by most advertisers. Of course, things were much simpler back then because people had not been overloaded on ads like they are today, but even so, a good ad will still tap into these basic pillars:

1. Reciprocity. This is one of the oldest tricks in the books of advertising - and it refers to making people feel like they owe something because they have done something for you. For example, if you go to a bar and they offer peanuts on the house, you will be much more likely to stay there for the evening, precisely because you feel you have been offered something for free and you want to *reciprocate* that.

Even more, you will actually feel the need to tip the servers - precisely because you feel that they have personally done a service to you by bringing you the *free* peanuts.

Of course, you are very much aware of why the bar is doing that. But even so, your natural tendency will be to pay them in the same coin and help them (and the servers) succeed.

How does this work with advertising? Just think of the thousand and one ads that offer a free gift - or the hundreds of digital products that offer a free trial. As a consumer, you want to get the most for your money, and companies that offer *freebies* will actually offer you more. In turn, you will want to reciprocate and stick with them for the satisfaction of your needs and desires.

2. Scarcity. You may not have perceived it this way, but scarcity is a tactic that is so common that almost every company uses it at one point or another. Put in simple terms, scarcity is all about the rarity or the time-related availability of a product.

Buy now, we're running out of it is the underlying message of every ad based on scarcity. And as silly as it may seem when you understand the basic technique behind it, as successful this tactic is.

The less of a product there is on the market, the more people will be likely to pay more and act fast. One of the best examples in this direction is the way haute couture fashion is made and sold: in very limited examples, for one season only.

The same goes with any kind of product that is advertised to be limited - or any kind of product whose pricing point is advertised to be limited. People are urged into buying something *because it will run out* and they don't want to be left on the outside of the game because they didn't take the opportunity (chance, as Aristotle named it) when it came.

3. Emotional appeal. This is by far one of the most complex techniques to use as an advertiser. While reciprocity and scarcity are fairly easy in terms of messaging, emotional appeal can be tricky to nail the right way. Do it right, and people will flock to your product precisely because it tickles their senses. It might be something related to the fact that they are not fit enough, or they don't have enough time, or they aren't successful enough, or simply something that taps into their desire to eat something comforting after a bad day at work.

Whatever you sell, chances are that you can tap into people's emotional needs to associate your product with a solution or ailment.

Done wrong, however, this type of ad can trigger snickers behind your back, complete ignoration of your products, or downright refusal to accept them.

This circles back to really knowing your audience and really knowing how to choose your words and your graphics to relay a very specific message that calls the audience you are targeting. To be frank, this is specifically why copywriters and graphic designers exist: because they have specialized into creating unique *forms* for messages that have been said already.

This is not to say that you cannot create amazing Facebook ads that tap into your audience's emotional appeal on your own. But you do have to take your time to understand that everyone is triggered by emotions - some decisions are rational, indeed. But a lot of them aren't - and when you understand how to create opportunity in that small corridor that leads to your audience's heart, you have won the game.

There are a million examples on how advertisers use this tactic - but if you want to think of something specific, think of every Coca-Cola ad and how it elicits happiness, good mood, and energy. That's what the brand has been associated with since its very beginnings - and that's the kind of emotions their ads trigger - including the famous *Christmas* truck ad that automatically makes you think of winter holiday (an ad so successful and powerful that everyone in the world can relate to it, even when they don't have specific winter holidays to celebrate in their cultures).

Sometimes, the emotions of people are triggered by physiology. Others, it's all about the big thoughts (like in the most recent Gillette ad, tapping into the #MeToo movement that has been going around on social media for the past year or so).

Sometimes, the product advertised is directly shown in the images. Other times, the specific product is not even shown - it is simply implied.

There could be entire books and libraries written about the emotional appeal of ads - both historically and on a contemporary level, both in traditional advertising and in digital advertising.

The key takeaway is that emotions trigger people to associate your product with one value or another - and that's a genuine gold mine right there: being able to make people feel good or be better with your ads (and subconsciously, with your *products*).

It doesn't matter what you sell, how you do it, or how much money you can invest in Facebook ads: sooner or later, it will all come down to one of the five groups of human needs and one of the seven causes for human action.

The key lies in both understanding how these needs work and in how you can create ad campaigns that really tap into these needs and triggers for action.

It is very important to keep in mind that people are not easily convinced. If you look back at the ads they made at the turn of the century and even late into the middle of the century (yes, the Mad Men era included), they were all rather puerile if you see them with the eyes of a modern consumer.

They were very simple in essence: they relayed a problem and offered a solution. Sometimes, the simplest words and the simplest explanations were used. Need better skin? No worries, this soap can do that for you because it has x, y, z ingredients that will help you do that. Need a new car? This Volkswagen Beetle with automatic transmission is so easy to drive that it can be driven by your wife too (yes, this ad actually exists!).

The graphics and pictures behind the written message (which was frequently quite long and tiresome for a modern reader) were very basic too. Sometimes, the product was associated with graphics or photos of smiling people (including in ads for cigarettes). Other times, the meaning of the image and text was on the more connotative side (i.e. the meaning was hidden under a humorous layer, for example).

But most of the time, those ads tapped into the audience back then: an audience that was much more likely to believe in ads, especially when a "specialist" was brought along (just think of toothpaste commercials that went way into the 2000s, where an *actor* dressed as a dentist would pop up recommending a certain brand).

These days, convincing your audience is much more difficult, and for a number of reasons:

- They have heard it all before, a gazillion times even

- They have the internet at their fingertips to *Google* everything

- They are just innately more skeptical, precisely because bad advertising has made them so

On top of this, it is very likely that you are targeting a Millennial audience too (i.e. people born between the 1980s and late 1990s-early 2000s in the largest acceptance of the term). Millennials crave for more than just the satisfaction of a need and desire - they need to believe in the products they buy and the products they themselves recommend to their peers. They need to test things, they need to see the inner workings, they need to be convinced - and they do all this because they know that, as consumers, the power is in their hands.

Lose weight fast-type of messages simply don't work anymore. You need to go beyond that and persuade your future customers in witty ads that are flawlessly designed to catch their attention (because, as mentioned before, most people do not pay attention to *anything* online for more than a few seconds).

That's where the *art* and *technology* of it all come together.

As an advertiser in the modern age, you cannot afford to be just a good salesperson, a brilliant copywriter, or a talented graphic designer. You need all of that and, to top it off, you need to have solid technical knowledge of how the internet works and how the major channels of communication work.

This book has been dedicated to the intricacies of Facebook advertising - but, as I was saying earlier on, knowing the technicalities is simply not enough. It makes for about 50% of the success rate of an ad - the rest is all persuasion, art, and knowing your audience and product like the back of your hand.

I will dedicate the last two sections of this book to help you bring together the *artistic* and the *technical* part of Facebook ads, as well as to inspire you by giving some brilliant examples of Facebook ad campaigns that actually worked (and *why* they were so successful).

Specific Advertising Tactics that Work on All Channels

Digital advertising has its specificities, sure - and Facebook ads do too. When it comes down to digging deep into the essence of how successful ads are made, however, the channel becomes less important as long as you know how it works and how to make the most out of it.

I want to take a bit of time to relay some of the most common (and efficient!) advertising tactics that work on every channel, regardless of product, industry, or audience. These tactics are not so much related to the strategy of how an ad is created, but they are actual hands-on, actionable techniques that can be applied online and offline, on every channel there is.

There are three major elements in every ad: the image, the branding, and the medium. Since we're talking about Facebook ads in this book and since this section is dedicated to tips that work on all media/channels, I will skip the last element and focus on the first two, as well as some adjacent components meant to make your ads even better.

How to Use Images in Advertising

Some images are better than others, but I am not here to debate that. Instead, let me show you some universally-valid techniques that have been applied since the very beginning of advertising itself:

1. Images on the left side of the ad. This is actual science right here. As you may know, the human brain is split

into two hemispheres: the left one dealing with the rational part of thinking and the right one dealing with the creative and emotional side. Oddly enough, the right side of the brain controls the left side of the body and the other way around (this is the main reason left-handed people are usually more creative). So, when an image is positioned on the left side of an ad, your right side will be the one processing it faster (ergo, you will be more likely to make an emotional decision - and one that is faster because the right side of your brain will process the information faster).

2. Whenever you show products in your ads, make sure they encourage action. There is a very simple example here: if you sell mugs, use pictures with the handle facing the right side because most people are right-handed and this will trigger a mental image/action of them actually holding the mug. The same goes with clothing images as well - the reason they are usually depicted on actual human models is that it helps you picture yourself wearing them. The same goes with shoes, which should be facing the viewer with the opening, or food products, which should be taken out of the package because it helps people create a mental image of eating them.

3. If you use human models in your pictures, make them look towards the call-to-action. This will immediately trigger viewers to look towards the call-to-action as well, making it more likely that they actually read it.

4. Use attractive models. Whenever you use human models for your ads, be sure to use attractive people. This might sound odd and it might be debatable in many contexts, but in general, you want to use pictures of attractive

people. They don't necessarily have to be top models (especially in today's context and especially when you are selling beauty or fashion products), but they do have to emanate a state of well-being, success, and happiness. Keep in mind that it is important to only use this technique where it makes sense. For instance, if you sell furniture or small appliances, it may not be the best tactic to include in your strategy.

5. If some words in your message are meant to trigger emotion, use larger fonts for it. Doing this will help people focus on the very essence of your ad (and what you want them to focus on, actually). Do keep in mind that you don't want to overuse this technique - it is one of those which have been used *way* too much and you want to be balanced in your approach of it.

6. Use assertive words - but be very cautious when and how you do it. Sometimes, assertive language can be perceived as too aggressive and it will generate an opposite effect in your target audience. One of the main areas where you *do* want to use assertive language is when selling so-called *hedonic* products (or products that are generally perceived as "indulgences", like chocolate, ice cream, wine, and so on).

7. Use rhymes for your tagline. OK, this might one can get really kitschy and cheesy, so it's really important to only use it where it makes sense and where your target audience is open to it. Used right, rhymes can make your tagline or motto more memorable and they can stick to people's brains, making it more likely that they will end up buying the product next time they stumble upon it.

How to Use Branding Marks and Logos in Advertising

Adding a logo or a brand to your ads is really important because you want people to associate that ad (and the emotion it instills or the need it fulfills) with your specific brand. Here are some of the basic tips in this category:

1. Your brand should be located on the right side. While images have to fall on the left side of an ad, branding marks should be located on the right side. Why? Because the left side of the brain will be unconsciously assimilating your logo or branding mark - so that it remembers it and recognizes it later on.

2. Find the right logo size. A logo or branding mark that is too small will make it virtually invisible - but one that's too large will make it too obnoxious and it will make people feel they are *too* advertised to.

How to Use the Best Visuals for Your Ads

In addition to images and logos, your ad will include other types of visuals as well - such as fonts and colors, which can trigger powerful reactions in people. More specifically, keep these tips in mind:

1. If you sell beauty products (or simply want to convey beauty), use fonts that are lightweight, thin, and long. Why? Because most people associate beauty with these characteristics, and they will overlay their perception of beauty on the fonts you use.

2. If your products are unique, use typefaces that are less common. It helps people associate your products with

your originality.

3. If you want to convey urgency and speed, slanted lettering can help. It will make your audience think that everything is *in a rush*, and thus, create a sense of urgency in them.

4. Use red when you want to draw preventive attention. Most people will read warnings that contain red because for decades and even centuries, red has been used in such contexts - so you can apply the same semantic meaning to your red-colored ad too.

5. When you describe the benefits offered by your product, use blue. This is usually connected to approachability and trustworthiness. To put this in comparison with the previous tip, imagine an ad saying "Our product will lead to X, Y, Z" on red, and then on blue. Doesn't it feel like the red one is a warning, rather than a list of benefits, and that the blue one creates a sense of trust?

6. Don't overdo it with the color, especially when there is a lot of text. Color attracts and makes your ads more interesting, but when you use too much of it, people might escape the very essence of the ad itself - and when that essence is encapsulated in text, you risk completely missing out on the opportunity to send a message.

Further Tips for Successful Ads

There are a couple of other tips you might want to consider when creating ads (for Facebook or any other channel, for that matter), namely:

1. If your market is new, the best way to go is by using a

rational approach - tapping into their needs and giving clear arguments on why your product is so good for these people.

2. If your market is old, the best way to go is by using an emotional approach - tapping into your target audience's desires and passions, more exactly.

3. Use a negative emotion when your product offers a solution to a very stringent issue. For instance, if you sell planning software, you can use something like "Don't let time run out of your hands" to show your audience your software can help with a stringent pain in their lives.

4. Use a positive emotion when you want people to remember you and your brand. Using the same example as above, if you sell a planning software, you can use something like "Let us help you plan better" if you want to help your audience remember you as a kind, warm brand voice.

5. Use variations of your ads. This is where Facebook truly excels because it allows you to segment and target different audiences with different ads and variations of an ad. For instance, if you sell a unisex perfume, you will still want to use images containing women when targeting women and images containing men when targeting men. This helps make your ads more relatable (and thus more likely to actually trigger action in your target audience).

6. Don't display your ad too many times. It makes people feel annoyed and overwhelmed - and those are two emotions you *don't* want to instill in your target audience no matter who they are or what you sell.

Of course, these are just some of the absolute basics of the world of advertising. Using them can completely change the way your ads are perceived - and when you combine all this knowledge with the power of Facebook ad targeting, you can really boost your sales and get an amazing ROI with your Facebook campaigns.

Bringing it All Together: The Scientific Know-How and the Art

You may think that this last chapter of the book was nothing but babbling nonsense that was not connected to Facebook ads in any way.

That is not true, however.

As I have iterated and reiterated it throughout the book, advertising is not really a science, and it's not really an art. It has never been - but today, in the digital age, the gap between the *technicalities* and the *art* is even slimmer than ever before.

At their very core, the specificities of Facebook advertising lie in knowing how to use the two most important features they offer:

- Ultra-targeting (I like to say "ultra" because it really is more specific than anything you could ever do with traditional advertising and it is more accurate and generous than many of the digital advertising channels as well)

- Custom audiences (which you can create based on a multitude of factors, including previous audiences you have successfully targeted and audiences that have been in touch - one way or another - with your website, your events, or simply, your product).

I will make an in-depth revision of the basic concepts in the *Conclusion* of this book. For now, however, I want to help you understand how science and art come together to create Facebook ads that work (I cannot emphasize the "that work" part enough, really).

Great Facebook ad campaigns happen when:

- You know how Facebook ads work (described in the first chapters of this book)

- You know how humans work (described in the first half of the second chapter)

- You know how ads in general work (described in the second half of the second chapter and tightly tied into the first half as well).

So, amazing, successful, click-driven, and conversion-driven Facebook ads can be created only when you have a very good understanding of what this platform offers, how to use it, and how to target the people you want to target. Once that level is covered, creating an ad that actually engages them is extremely important.

Why?

Because you can have the best targeting skills - if your ad is bland and it says nothing, it will only be shown to the right people, but they will not be moved by it.

That is pretty much the same as selling your products at the farmer's market without cleaning them first. You're in the right place, and people willing to buy this kind of product are there. You find a good table right at the entrance so that people see you. But when they stumble upon your products, they notice your tomatoes are muddy and your sign is torn apart.

Will they buy from you?

Most likely, no. They do want *bio*products, but they also want their products to be minimally appealing. Not perfect, but appealing. They want to picture those tomatoes sliced up and in a salad, not picture themselves heavily cleaning them when they go home.

Knowing about the way Facebook works is crucial because it will help you narrow down your segment and show your ads to as many potential buyers interested in the group of products you sell as you can.

At the same time, though, knowing how to craft engaging ads will help you make sure those ads are not just *seen*, but *actioned upon* as well.

Is there a recipe for it?

No, precisely because all products are unique in their own way, all markets are unique, and all target audiences are unique as well.

There are, however, *ingredients* that will make your ad campaigns more successful - just like salt and pepper are at the foundation of most dishes.

It's all about the blend and the balance - you can't make do without the technical side, but you can't completely ignore the basics of good advertising either. The balance is somewhere between the two: between the market research and the targeting, between the understanding of your product and the understanding of your audience, between technical and artistic.

Inspirational Examples of Brilliant Ad Campaigns

The internet is filled with really bad advertising.

You'll spot the very bad one from a mile - it usually drags you in without notice, it offers nothing but the picture of a "successful human being", and then brings in an ad copy that's mediocre at its best and absolutely horrible at its worst.

You know them, you have seen them every step of the way.

There used to be a time when the internet was all about these ads.

As tools and audiences have evolved, however, this kind of ads are less and less noticeable on reputable sites (like Facebook ads, for example). They will pop up every now and again, but they are rarer and rarer with every day.

What does this mean for you as a future advertiser on Facebook?

On the one hand, it means that you can do awesome things. If you love digital marketing and advertising, this is one of the best times to get in-depth with this because it will help you create campaigns you will proudly look back on.

On the other hand, it also means that the general quality of online ads is improving - so you need to step up your game if you want to make sure your ads yield actual results.

This is why I insisted so much on bringing forward more than just Facebook techniques: the internet (and Facebook in particular) is filled with people who can use the tool, but can't use the basics of good advertising. So, if you want your ads to be really good, you need to really work this out (and you do want your ads to be good, if not for anything else, then just for the mere fact that you're investing serious financial resources in this).

What are some of the very best and most successful ad campaigns on Facebook?

I've picked two of them for you, to exemplify the way they work and how it is that they are so successful.

Allbirds - A Simple Video Ad

This ad is magnificent for a long list of reasons. It's simple, yet ultra-effective, and it taps into the exact needs of the product's target audience.

For a bit of context, this brand sells shoes - and the ad itself shows two feet, with the brand's shoes on, moving around.

It just doesn't get simpler than this: it's straight to the point, it's easy, it's clean, and it's focused.

The ad copy says "Machine washable, for when life gets dirty".

And the text above the ad says "I can't say enough about how comfortable these shoes are. Free shipping and free returns". [7]

All of this is topped off with a simple and to the point call to action: "Buy Now".

---

[7] Bernazzani, S. (2019). 13 of the Best Facebook Ad Examples That Actually Work (And Why). Retrieved from https://blog.hubspot.com/blog/tabid/6307/bid/33319/10-examples-of-facebook-ads-that-actually-work-and-why.aspx

Just like that.

The ad meets all the criteria to be a great one:

- It has great visuals (and, surprise-surprise, there's no color in this!)

- It is relevant (because it shows to people who are interested in shoes)

- It offers value (it says the shoes are comfortable, washable, and they come with free delivery)

- The call to action is straight on point.

Grammarly - A Story Video Ad

Although attention span on the internet tends to be really low, this doesn't mean that slightly longer video ads aren't feasible.

As long as they are done right, these ads can entice, attract, keep, and convert an audience.

This Grammarly ad takes the prize in terms of using storytelling to connect their brand with a beautiful story.

Basically, it is the story of a sushi chef who teaches sushi making lessons. On the side, he writes a blog and he uses Grammarly to check his grammar.

This might sound very basic. But the ad is so well made from a visual point of view and the story is so emotional that you get drawn into it. [8]

---

[8]The 5 Best Facebook Ad Campaigns That Killed It In 2018. (2019). Retrieved from https://adespresso.com/blog/best-facebook-ad-campaigns/

Basically, this brand awareness ad meets all quality standards on all levels:

- it is highly visual (which, as we have established, is always attractive)

- it is relevant (it is shown to writers and people who use English in communication)

- it triggers an emotion (the emotion of someone who is successful and shares their passion with the world)

- it ties into the brand itself.

Simple, clean, beautiful.

The fact that I have chosen two video ads to exemplify is both coincidental and not so much.

On the one hand, video works. It is clearly easier to send a message and get your audience's attention with video than it is with a lot of text (as we have discussed before, it's just the way the brain is wired).

On the other hand, it is very important to note that video is not the *only* example that works.

There are hundreds and hundreds of Facebook ads formatted as anything else than video - and they work.

The point here is that your ads need to bring together all the information I have presented to you until now.

Without the technical part, you're spending a lot of money and knocking on the wrong doors.

Without the artistic part, you're spending a lot of money and not opening any doors.

Amazing Facebook ads are out there - open your eyes, do your research, and take your time with the understanding of all the concepts described in this book. Hell, do some cheap tests and extrapolate them if you need to do things with your own hands to see how it works.

Most importantly, do not be afraid to think out of the box.

That's where the true value of an ad lies: in working your way out of the little ad square Facebook has designed for you and stepping into people's lives by 1) targeting them correctly and 2) speaking to them correctly.

Facebook Ads and GDPR

Now, this is an iffy topic for those of you just starting out in digital marketing - and a downright traumatizing one for anyone who was around in anything digital marketing-related back in May 2018.

GDPR is a serious issue, though.

If you are targeting anyone in the European Union, you absolutely have to abide by it.

This is not just "good practice" - it's actual legislation, with a regulatory body, and with fines that could put your business into the ground if you don't follow the rules.

This is by no means meant to scare you off.

It's meant to:

- Help you protect yourself against the repercussions of not following GDPR

- Practice better, more ethical marketing

GDPR might be a headache to implement, but at the end of the day, it is to everyone's benefit that you do it - and not just because you're scared to be fined, but also because GDPR actually helps you be more transparent with your audience. Transparency leads to trust - and trust leads to conversion, retention, and evangelism.

Regardless of how you look at it, GDPR is something to follow - even when you don't specifically target European citizens.

What Is GDPR?

GDPR stands for General Data Regulation Protection.

This might not say much, but digital marketing has been the most affected area in terms of implementations that need to adhere to GDPR. Of course, the data protection regulation did expand to offline marketing as well - because as you may very well know it, both offline and online marketing rely *a lot* on collecting data about consumers and using it for future campaigns.

GDPR affects multiple types of data, including the following:

- Information related to the identity of a person (name, address, ID numbers)

- Information related to web data (location, IP address, cookies, and so on)

- Information related to health and genetics

- Information related to race and ethnicity

- Information related to political views

- Information related to sexual orientation

As a marketer, you might have to store, manage, and analyze any of the aforementioned type of data - and this includes marketing on Facebook as well. Therefore, GDPR will affect your business and you do need to adhere to its rules.

You might think that you don't have to abide by these regulations if you don't specifically target EU citizens. However, that is not true: the internet is a free space and people from Europe might land on your site (and have their cookies stored) and they might subscribe to your newsletter even if you don't specifically target them.

Because this book is dedicated to Facebook advertising, I will only relay the important GDPR rules to know in connection to this - but do keep in mind that GDPR applies to pretty much any other form of internet marketing and/or advertising.

In a nutshell, this is what GDPR means for Facebook advertisers:

- You need to make sure your subscribers that you will use their data (and how)

- You need people to give their specific consent for you to use their data. Do keep in mind that they are free to withdraw said consent whenever they feel like it too

- You need to show your customers the data you have stored about them when and if they require it

- You need to allow users to edit their information any time they want (and any kind of information you may be storing about them too)

- You need to allow users to delete the information you have stored about them whenever they want

How Does GDPR Affect the Facebook Pixel?

As shown in the previous chapters of this book, the Facebook pixel is a line of code that allows you to "track" your users' activity with the purpose of targeting them for future ad campaigns on this specific platform.

If you use the Facebook pixel, you are automatically obliged to comply with the General Data Protection Regulation.

Let's take some common examples of when and how this should be done:

- If you run an eCommerce store and use cookies to collect data about the pages/ products users view, you have to inform them of this, so that they know they will be shown ads that suit the data collected by your site

- If you have a blog that has some form of analytics on it, the demographic information about the readers is collected through cookies - so you should comply with GDPR

- If you run a news media site and you use any kind of third-party server to display ads, that third-party server uses cookies to collect information about users who view those ads - so, again, you need to comply with GDPR

- If you are a Facebook advertiser and you have installed either the Facebook or the Atlas pixel on your site, your visitors need to be informed of this. They need to be able to opt out of it, and they need to be explained that the pixel data will be used to measure ad conversions, as well as to generate retargeting campaigns on Facebook

Do keep in mind that *consent* is a very important aspect of GDPR. The way most websites have done this is by implementing a pop-up or overlay that clearly specifies the terms of the site, the way the cookies are used, and then give options to readers: either opt in or opt out of this. There are free tools to install on your site to help you with this, so with a bit of research, it should be actually easy.

The installation of the plugin is not the most painful part for a marketer, though: offering people the option to *not* be used in retargeting campaigns means that they will not be able to be retargeted (or targeted, to begin with). On the one hand, this helps you narrow down your audience to people who actually want to see your offers. On the other hand, this might narrow down your audience a bit too much.

Either way, you still **absolutely have to abide by GDPR.**

How Does GDPR Affect Facebook Custom Audiences?

Along with the pixel, custom audiences make Facebook a very good place for any kind of online advertiser.

However, custom audiences are too subjected to GDPR.

Let's say, for example, that you have an email list and you want to upload it to Facebook to use it in your targeting campaigns. This is a custom audience based on data you already have - but even so, by uploading it to Facebook, you become a data controller. And, according to GDPR, as a data controller, you need to ask your subscribers for their consent before you can create campaigns geared at them.

If you have already uploaded any kind of list with data on it on Facebook for your campaigns, you need to delete it and start anew, by asking people for their consent.

Also, do make sure you regularly clean out your custom audience lists on Facebook, to make sure you remove those users who have withdrawn their consent.

How Does GDPR Affect Facebook Lookalike Audiences?

Last, but definitely not least, GDPR affects the way you work with the Facebook lookalike audience feature as well.

In theory, lookalike audiences should not be affected by GDPR - mostly because the mechanism behind this feature uses a "seed" audience of a custom audience you have already created - so technically, you are not holding any kind of information about your audience, neither are maneuvering it in any way.

However, my advice is to play on the safe side and update your privacy policy according to GDPR even if you only use lookalike audiences.

Is it really *that* bad if you don't abide by GDPR?

Well, yes. Regulators are very keen on making this the absolute Bible of internet data privacy - and they are going to be very serious about companies who don't abide by the rules too. Even if you are a small player, you are still liable to pay huge fines for not following GDPR.

Is that worth it?

No, it's better to err on the safe side and be ready. With the Facebook scandal last year, and with GDPR being in full swing since May 2018, you really have no excuse not to abide by GDPR anymore.

Conclusion

I'm sure this entire book has been a rollercoaster for you - especially if Facebook ads (and ads in general) are something relatively new in your life.

Even if you were at least vaguely familiar with how Facebook ads work and how to really make the most out of every single ad you publish, I still hope that this book has taught you one or two new things.

When I started writing this, I meant to really offer you the best fu*king guide on Facebook advertising - and to do this, I felt the need to walk you through both the specifics of Facebook as a channel of communication and through the theoretical and practical know-how of creating ads that *make it happen*.

I started off with some of the elements that make Facebook advertising really stand out - both when compared with traditional marketing and digital marketing. Sure, other channels do offer targeting options and sure, they are great when your target audience is there. But truly, no other channel offers you an audience of more than 2.3 billion people, which you can very specifically target according to very specific interests, demographics, behaviors, and so on.

Facebook has mastered the art of bringing technical knowledge into the hands of modern advertisers.

In 2018, when Mark Zuckerberg stood in front of the Congress and was asked how come he makes money with a platform that is essentially free, he answered simply: *Senator, we run ads.* [9]

---

[9] Abbruzzese, J. (2019). 'We run ads'. Retrieved from https://www.nbcnews.com/card/we-run-ads-n864606

That's the very essence of Facebook encapsulated in four simple words.

This entire platform is a means by which people interact with each other. It can be used to post all the cat videos in the world, or it can be used as an immensely powerful tool to target your specific audience. With practice, good advertising skills (which I'll get to in a moment), and some money, you can get your product out there.

And I need to re-emphasize this again: you can get your product out there to that specific slice of the 2.3 billion people cake that is likely to actually buy your product as well.

The core of Facebook lies in its ads: so it makes all the sense in the world that they will offer a very comprehensive and detailed platform for advertisers to run their ads.

Facebook has been a complete game changer for the world of online ads - and although targeted ads have existed before, never before have they been so intimate, so close to the target audience, and so easy to segment at the same time.

My intuition is saying that Facebook will survive and that their ad platform will get even better in time. But, as they say, time itself will tell.

Targeting, custom audiences, the (in)famous Facebook pixel - these technicalities make Facebook a worthy ally for every marketer. It doesn't matter if you sell luxury shoes or tractors: your audience is most likely on Facebook, and this is where they feel "at home" because this is where their families and friends are, even when they are thousands of miles away.

When you run ads on Facebook, you basically get the chance to enter a space people perceive as very personal and very public at the same time. *This* is where the true power of the platform lies, along with its targeting capabilities and its audience building options.

At the same time, it is crucial to acknowledge that Facebook ads are absolutely nothing if you don't create them with a good sense of what you need and what your audience needs from the very beginning.

If you enter someone's house and force them into buying your toaster, you're losing the game before you have even won.

If, however, you hear someone needs a new toaster, you offer them a serving, and then present your new model, you're in for the win.

Great ads happen when you understand the psychology of the buyer and what makes them tick. Great ads happen when you open the door to emotion or rational thought and when you know how to listen to your audience just as much as you know how to talk to them.

Great ads happen when no detail is too small to be omitted. When every full stop makes a difference and every pixel matters.

Great ads happen when you put your great mind to work.

Bibliography

30 ways to get more Facebook Ads clicks than you ever imagined - Connectio. (2019). Retrieved from https://connectio.io/30-ways-improve-facebook-ads-ctr/

(2019). Retrieved from https://www.researchgate.net/publication/254298719_Men_Women_and_Sports_Audience_Experiences_and_Effects

Abbruzzese, J. (2019). 'We run ads'. Retrieved from https://www.nbcnews.com/card/we-run-ads-n864606

Bernazzani, S. (2019). 13 of the Best Facebook Ad Examples That Actually Work (And Why). Retrieved from https://blog.hubspot.com/blog/tabid/6307/bid/33319/10-examples-of-facebook-ads-that-actually-work-and-why.aspx

Facebook users worldwide 2018 | Statista. (2019). Retrieved from https://www.statista.com/statistics/264810/number-of-monthly-active-facebook-users-worldwide/

Global Internet usage. (2019). Retrieved from https://en.wikipedia.org/wiki/Global_Internet_usage

Marvin, G. (2019). Survey: 3 Out Of 4 Consumers Now Notice Retargeted Ads - Marketing Land. Retrieved from https://marketingland.com/3-out-4-consumers-notice-retargeted-ads-67813

Shifts for 2020: Multisensory multipliers. (2019). Retrieved from https://www.facebook.com/business/news/insights/shifts-for-2020-multisensory-multipliers

The 5 Best Facebook Ad Campaigns That Killed It In 2018. (2019). Retrieved from https://adespresso.com/blog/best-facebook-ad-campaigns/

www.ingramcontent.com/pod-product-compliance
Lightning Source LLC
Chambersburg PA
CBHW050643190326
41458CB00008B/2401